Liberationships

A volume in
Identity & Practice in Higher Education–Student Affairs
Pietro A. Sasso and Shelley Price-Williams, *Series Editors*

Identity & Practice in Higher Education–Student Affairs

Pietro A. Sasso and Shelley Price-Williams, *Series Editors*

Institutional Diversity in American Postsecondary Education (2024)
   Tiffany J. Davis, Shelley Price-Williams, and Pietro A. Sasso

Affirming Identity, Advancing Belonging, and Amplifying Voice in Sororities and Fraternities (2024)
   Pietro A. Sasso, Mónica Lee Miranda, and J. Patrick Biddix

Latinx College Students: Innovations in Mental Health, Advocacy, and Social Justice Programs (2024)
   José Miguel Maldonado and Adrianne L. Johnson

Stir What You've Got: Insights From a College President (2023)
   William T. Greer Jr.

Identity in Supervision: Understanding Who Works for You and Who You Work for in Higher Education (2023)
   Roger 'Mitch' Nasser Jr.

Still Working While Black: The Untold Stories of Student Affairs Practitioners (2023)
   Antione D. Tomlin

Working While Black: The Untold Stories of Student Affairs Practitioners (2022)
   Antione D. Tomlin

Liberationships

Critical Mentorship in Practice

Kim McAloney
Oregon State University

Jenesis Rose Long
Augustana University

INFORMATION AGE PUBLISHING, INC.
Charlotte, NC • www.infoagepub.com

Library of Congress Cataloging-in-Publication Data

A CIP record for this book is available from the Library of Congress
http://www.loc.gov

ISBN: 979-8-88730-809-8 (Paperback)
　　　979-8-88730-810-4 (Hardcover)
　　　979-8-88730-811-1 (E-Book)

Copyright © 2025 Information Age Publishing Inc.

All rights reserved. No part of this publication may be reproduced, stored in a retrieval system, or transmitted, in any form or by any means, electronic, mechanical, photocopying, microfilming, recording or otherwise, without written permission from the publisher.

Printed in the United States of America

Contents

Foreword vii
Larry Roper, PhD

Acknowlegments xi

1 **How Did We Get Here?** 1
  Kim McAloney, PhD 2
  Jenesis Rose Long, EdM 6
  Mentorship and the Development of Liberationships 9

2 **Introduction to Liberatory Mentorship for Women of Color** 11
  Methodology 12
  Results 13
  Overview 13
  Who 14
  How 16
  Why 19
  How We Named the Model 22

3 **Mentorship Is More Than Meets the Eye** 23
  Coming Into Our Racial Selves 24
  The Evolution of Mentorships Into Liberationships 27
  Supervision 31

4 **Literature on Mentorship** 37
   Mentorship Among Women of Color 37
   Critical Pedagogy 49

5 **Why Mentorship?** 51
   Historical Context of Minoritized Communities
      Within Higher Education 51
   History of Women in Higher Education 56
   Essential Role of Transformative and Liberatory Relationships 58

6 **"Considerations and Recommendations"** 67
   Section 1: Considerations and Recommendations for Mentors 68
   Section 2: Considerations and Recommendations for Mentees 75

7 **Self-Reflection Activities and Worksheets** 81
   Activity 1: Critical Mentorship as Women of Color
      in Higher Education Worksheet 81
   Activity 2: Personal Reflection Questions 83
   Activity 3: Journal and Reflection Prompts 84
   Activity 4: Personal Identity Exploration 86
   Activity 5: Values Assessment 89
   Activity 6: Relationship Self-Care Inventory 92
   Activity 7: Identity-Affirming Reflection 94
   Activity 8: Liberationship Preferences 95
   Activity 9: Liberation in the Academy: Reflection Questions
      for Educators 98
   Activity 10: Reflection Questions to Use as You Begin Virtual
      Mentor or Liberationships for Implementation
      of Study Findings 100

Epilogue 105
   Gunnar Whisler

References 109

About the Authors 115

Foreword

Across our globe, throughout our nation, within states, communities and institutions people are seeking meaningful connections, life-giving relationships and personal nourishment. The desire for mutually loving relationships is a universal need and desire. At a more basic level, people have a need to be seen, heard, understood and valued. At the same time, as we grow from infancy to adulthood, implicitly or explicitly we wrestle with recurring questions about our identity, purpose and meaning—questions such as, "Who am I?"; "Why am I?"; "What do I hope to get done?"; and "What does the world most need from me?" Such profound questions, as the ones we are faced with in making meaning of our lives and navigating the journey towards the future that lie before us cannot be adequately addressed in isolation. If we are to grow into our full self, cultivate an authentic way of being, and follow a life course consistent with our most deeply held values, we must have the support and encouragement of others.

Within the sphere of higher education, individuals often rely upon those who they identify as mentors for support and guidance as they make crucial decisions about ways to reconcile life dilemmas, contemplate what paths to pursue and determine how to achieve one's desires. If we were to speak with most adults and query them about their path to success, most would cite the essential role that a mentor played in their growth and development. Mentoring relationships can be pivotal to those seeking direction and meaning. While mentoring, as most of us have experienced those relationships, can produce great value, traditional mentoring has its flaws. The construct under which traditional mentoring relationships operate can be quite limiting.

Mentoring is a relationship of choice, which means, most often the relationship is initiated by a person in a position of power or influence who uses their knowledge and status to benefit a younger person. In some cases, the prospective mentor identifies a person with whom they feel an affinity or who reminds them of a younger version of themselves and forge a relationship to help that person follow a career path similar to theirs. In other cases, a less experienced person may seek out the insights or wisdom of a more seasoned person and forge a mentoring relationship as a result of their initiative. Through both scenarios, some mentors will use their influence to mold a person into someone who is a newer form of themselves. This type of mentoring, while appearing magnanimous, can also be manipulative. Though I am sure that the vast majority of mentors sincerely believe that they are acting in the best interest of the mentee. I have no doubt that the preponderance of people who seek and desire mentoring are looking for a person who can support them in being the best possible version of their authentic self. Mentoring, as we know it now, has been meaningful and additive for many. Nonetheless, the diversity of our campuses and the uniqueness of the lives and personal strivings of those who walk the halls of colleges and universities makes it clear that we need to disrupt our current notion of mentoring and uncover possibilities for enhancing the agency of those receiving mentoring.

The current version of mentoring has led to an institutional environment in which those who do not resemble those in positions of power, influence and in control of institutional resources are generally overlooked and excluded. Particularly in institutions that lack demographic diversity, women of color are often disregarded when possibilities for mentorship are considered. This Euro-male influenced model must be interrupted and transformed.

In *Liberationships: Critical Mentorship in Practice*, Kim McAloney and Jenesis Long give us a model that not only disrupts and transforms our notion of mentoring, but also provides us with a model for reconsidering our responsibilities to those with whom we are in close relationship. It is especially significant that this model focuses on mentorship for women of color, given all that we know about the marginality, invisibility, voicelessness and oppression that far too many women of color experience in the Academy. In this book the authors introduce the concept of liberationships, which at its core challenges us to think about the power of having access to relationships or people in our life who free us up to live bravely, freely and in alignment with our spirit and soul. In their model they name dynamics that often go unspoken in traditional mentoring—power, identity difference or resonance, systemic norms and resistance, and White supremacy. Liberationships free up those involved in the relationship to name whatever is so for them, it allows each person, through their authentic voice to express their needs, desires, hopes and fears. Liberationships create space to name the ties that are binding one and provides connections to severe those unproductive constraints. Liberationships offer a mutuality and ethic of common caring that is not always visible in traditional mentoring interactions. McAloney and Long name, explain and provide a road map for what can be and should be in relationships committed to reciprocally nurturing the best in each other.

Liberationships: Critical Mentorship in Practice makes the case that developing liberationships and advancing one's growth begins with committing to doing the necessary internal work to become aware, including accessing the humility and vulnerability to accept that we have much to learn and that the needed learning can be facilitated through an intentionally liberating relationship. The authors demonstrate throughout that in mentoring relationships consciousness must precede action, that we must be conscious of the realities of others, if we are to engage with them with integrity. As this book demonstrates, awareness, reflection and action are strongly linked. When we fully engage, we are able to demonstrate our ability to listen and hear, understand and respond, sense and feel, and act on what we know. McAloney and Long leave no doubt that, if we embrace liberationships, remarkable personal transformation can take place (and ultimately, institutional and social transformation).

As you read this book, allow yourself to welcome and embrace the powerful call to rethink mentoring, as it has been presented to most of us. Consider the possibilities for what liberationships can offer you and those to whose success and well-being you are committed. In Chapter 7 the authors provide a compendium of powerful emotionally and intellectually stimulating questions and activities. The model and activities presented in this book demonstrate that creating nourishing, life-enriching relationships requires time, attention, care and thoughtfulness. The path to liberationship must include reframing our thinking, changing our behavior, and enhancing our awareness. Chapter 8 provides explicit guidance on how to create institutional programs to promote and support the success of minoritized community members. This guidance will support institutional leaders who carry a commitment to providing culturally appropriate and responsive mentoring to students and other community members who have been historically underserved and ill-served by traditional mentoring relationships.

This book is significant and groundbreaking, its contribution to higher education and specifically to the well-being of women of color cannot be under-estimated. This publication not only disrupts the traditional construct of mentoring, but also challenges hierarchy and the notions of White supremacy on which it is constructed. As I read this manuscript, I was reminded of the admonition Frantz Fanon (1963) issued to Black people in the United States and Africa in *Wretched of the Earth*:

> So, comrades, let us not pay tribute to Europe by creating states, institutions and societies which draw inspiration from her.
>
> Humanity is waiting for something from us other than such an imitation, which would be almost an obscene caricature.
>
> If we want to turn Africa into a new Europe, and America into a new Europe, then let us leave the destiny of our countries to Europeans. They will know how to do it better than the most gifted among us.
>
> But if we want humanity to advance a step further, if we want to bring it up to a different level than that which Europe has shown it, then we must invent and we must make discoveries. (p. 315)

This innovative, culturally-grounded work done by McAloney and Long point to a new way, a way that following the European-influenced, male-centered model of mentoring would never take us. By embracing and enacting their model we can, indeed, "advance humanity a step further."

—**Larry D. Roper, PhD**
Emeritus Professor of Language, Culture, and Society
Oregon State University

Acknowledgments

This book has been brought to life through the support, encouragement, and love of so many incredible people in our community.

To liberation leaders who have paved the way for this work to be continued: Janet Nishihara, Larry Roper, Mamta Accapadi, Cynthia Dillard, thank you for prioritizing what matters most—human connection. We carry your wisdom and insights with us into every conversation we have with our community members. You showed us how we can give of ourselves without sacrificing our humanity, how to love and lead, and how to speak up for those who need support. Thank you for your sacrifices and commitment to being a source of good in this world and through your careers.

To our students, including most notably Gunnar Whisler who wrote our epilogue, Jade Johnson who provided detailed edits on our work, and Sandra Cervantes who supported our literature review work: thank you for bringing hope and light into our lives by sharing your dreams and goals with us. It is a privilege to hold space for your visions and to support you as you bring about a better world. You inspire us to wake up every morning determined to continue serving and connecting with our community.

From Jenesis: to my friends and family, thank you for holding me through all of the change I navigated during 2024, the final year of work on this book. I could not have made it through without the love and care of my sister Krystle, my brother-in-law Sully, my best friends Kim and Michelle, and their families. To Jade Johnson, thank you for being my ideal reader, and for reminding me that things can continue to get better if I am brave enough to go after what I really want. To my little loves, Damien, Kaiya, and Jade, thank you for the regular reminders of how special it is to be alive and experiencing this world together. Please always remember, this world is ours to create.

From Kim: To my friends and family, thank you for holding space, always supporting, and believing in me. What a journey! Chad, Ella, and Diana, your joy, light, and smiles are precious. Thank you for lighting up this auntie's life! To Adam and Damien, living in your humanity (laughter and joy, curiosity, creativity, spaciousness and support of others) is home and the best place to be. Thank you for supporting my ever stretching dreams, for doing life together, and for doing the work. I love you infinity!

1

How Did We Get Here?

We, the authors, acknowledge that our journey to writing this book has been deeply shaped by not only our academic and professional lives, but also our personal lives. Given that, in this chapter, we will share about our exploration of mentorship through various experiences, and highlight many of the most influential experiences we've had during our liberationship that have brought us to the place where we are able to write this book. Liberationships are mutually beneficial relationships that empower all parties to reach their personally defined goals while addressing systemic barriers. Because of this interwoven dynamic of our liberationship, we are choosing to write this book in scholarly personal narrative (Nash & Viray, 2013), so we will add personal anecdotes and our lessons learned throughout it. We invite you to read this book through a holistic lens and consider its lessons through your multiple identities as an academic, professional, and multi-faceted human.

Kim McAloney, PhD

My first mentorship experiences were in the Christian church. I was mentored on what it meant to be a woman; namely, how to be a good, godly wife and mother. I also learned to engage with and support others in the community largely by sharing what I have and to use my organization and planning skills to help others learn, grow, and engage in experiences. While this was foundational to my life, something was missing.

Fast forward through life experiences supporting my shifting narrative and experience with organized religion, my first collegiate experience was at a community college where I knew just a few students. I attended both on campus and correspondence courses, as we called them then. I had engagement with some of my faculty, but felt largely disconnected from campus and the institution. I took some time off school given life experiences and was encouraged to pick it up again when we moved for my partner's transfer from community college to university. Taking his advice, I set up a meeting with the education academic advisor at what would be our new local community college. After her and my conversation, the advisor walked me over to the TRIO Student Support Services office where I not only applied for the program, but was offered a work study position as an office assistant given my past work experience. Through the TRIO Student Support Services program not only did I receive academic counseling, but support from my student community. As a group, we felt not represented by the current student government and decided to write one another in on the student government ballot during elections. This community organizing led me to be elected as a student representative. Little did I know that that experience would drastically shape my career and life.

It was in this student representative leadership role that I met a mentor who changed so much for me. This mentor, the student government advisor, was Tammi Paul. She was an amazing, thoughtful, caring, and supportive advisor. She listened to where we wanted to go as a team, and individually, and then supported us in the journey to achieving those goals. One day, Tammi, knowing I was interested in working in education, asked me if I had considered working in higher education as I seemed to really enjoy student government work. I'd wanted to work in education, though I was thinking of working with preschoolers at this time. Tammi connected me with Dr. Larry Roper at Oregon State University (OSU). At that time, Larry was the vice provost for student affairs at OSU and was teaching Black Identity Development through the ethnic studies, one of my two majors in my transfer to the university the next term which I decided to enroll in.

Larry's class was engaging. I talked about things in that class I'd never discussed before: My identity as a Black bi/multiracial person. I met a few other students who were biracial. These conversations were affirming in ways that took me years to be able to name. At the end of the class, Larry asked me what I wanted to do in my career. I shared my interest in considering student affairs and working in higher education. Directly following our meeting, he connected me to an internship program at Oregon State University which was the university I was dual enrolled in along with my community college, and to the NAPSA Undergraduate Fellows Program (NUFP) a semi-structured mentorship program for minoritized students through the student affairs administrator organization NASPA to explore this professional pathway. As OSU's NUFP had a campus community, I also was able to connect with Dr. Mamta Accapadi, OSU's dean of students at that time. When making my full transition from finishing at community college and transferring to OSU, I also connected with OSU's TRIO Student Support Services program and the state-funded Educational Opportunities Program (EOP) that began out of a Black student walk about 40 years before I arrived. It was here, within EOP, that I met Dr. Janet Nishihara, the program's director.

A Different Kind of Leadership

Larry Roper, Mamta Accapadi, and Janet Nishihara. I was struck by each of them: the way they engaged and treated people. Each of them are very different people and yet these core feelings and actions I saw and experienced from each of them were different than any I had experienced before. They were genuine, authentic, and themselves; not a single story I got from the church where I was consistently shown how to be a White, middle-class values wife and mom. These core characteristics of building community, holding people's humanity, and engaging in authentic and transparent leadership were there in each of them, but all three engage with these characteristics in their own way. They care about justice and its birth from a place of love. Each believes in other people's humanity and works to create a more just world in ways I had not experienced anywhere else. It was in this space at the cross-section of learning more about myself as a racialized being, in relationship with these beautiful humans and leaders who engage in the world that made me feel like I could not only bring my full self, but also that I had something to contribute, and who, from this core, expressed leadership in different ways, began connecting pieces for me. I was able to take the core components I held dear from Christianity around justice, love, and community and was able to bring my full new understandings of myself and my communities to help me embrace my whole self and begin to dream about how I can lead authentically.

As I wrapped up my undergraduate experience, I was able to engage in a formal mentorship relationship with Larry through the NUFP program. I volunteered as a teaching assistant for an ethnic studies course that Mamta taught. I had an unofficial mentorship with Janet as when I joined EOP, she assigned me a different academic counselor than herself so we could talk about the overlapping interest we both had in ethnic studies and student affairs. Janet encouraged and mentored me through submitting my first conference proposal to the NASPA Multicultural Institute which was accepted and co-presented with her.

As I transitioned into my master's program in OSU's college student services administration (CSSA) program, Larry became my major advisor and committee chair. Mamta became my assistantship supervisor and Janet and I worked together through a summer bridge extended orientation program for first year, first generation, low income, and rural college students. With this transition from undergraduate to graduate student and then, again, to professional, my relationship with Mamta and Janet shifted. As I transitioned roles from graduate student to professional, Mamta, who remained my supervisor, and Janet, who I continued working and teaching with, began sharing with me differently at each of these transition points. As this sharing shifted, so did our mentorship relationships. While they didn't dramatically shift, my connection then with Larry and Mamta was different than with Janet. With my class-of-origin being working class and poor, I held their positions as vice provost for student affairs and dean of students, respectively, with a bit of distance. While they created the space for us to continue to shift and deepen our mentorship relationships, I was confined by my limited thinking and epistemological frame within racial capitalism. They were each in such high positions of the university and here I am just a grad student and new professional. With Janet, however, though she was the director of EOP, I felt more open to her as the director position felt like a smaller structural barrier to overcome, allowing for a deeper connection; and we, together, formed a liberationship. Even with my own limiting views of our mentorship at the time, each of these experiences with Larry, Mamta, and Janet helped shape how I come to know, how I show up, and how I understand mentorship and the liberatory possibilities through education today.

Epistemological and Pedagogical Foundations

My professional journey has led me to work with the dean of students office, in academic support programs, and in coordinating higher education and student affairs graduate programs. Each of these roles have continued to shape who I am and how I engage with students, colleagues, and society. It was the dean of students office under Mamta's recommendation that first introduced me to both *Sentipensante* pedagogy (Rendón, 2008) and hooks' (1998) engaged pedagogy. These pedagogies shape how I see my role as an educator which includes mentorship and supervision. I have had the opportunity and support to experiment with and solidify what these pedagogies mean and could mean for my professional practice. I have served as a mentor for about a dozen undergraduate students through the NUFP, which is how I was able to first meet, connect, and build this liberationship with Jenesis.

Throughout my professional roles, I have been able to serve students through academic counseling. Academic counseling is holistic advising recognizing that a student's academics are impacted by their other identities and roles (as possible siblings, children, roommates, students of color, employees, etc.). This work of holding, viewing, and working with people holistically have helped me in my formation of what mentorship could fully be and have allowed me to push the bounds of what it meant to be an academic counselor/advisor, supervisor, mentor, and instructor. Working in the academic support program helped me continue to hone these pedagogies through my engagement with students and colleagues both in and out of the unit.

Over the course of my decade plus in the profession, I have had the opportunity to serve as an internships supervisor for several dozen undergraduate and graduate students including Jenesis. I had the opportunity to build an internship program within the dean of students office that supported both NUFP and other undergraduates exploring careers in student affairs as well as higher education and student affairs graduate students. One of my early professional roles was to support graduate students enrolled in a higher education master's program, first, providing direct student support, and then as a program administrator, advisor, graduate committee member, and instructor. I was able to use engaged pedagogy and *sentipensante* pedagogy within and outside of the classroom. I was able to use these pedagogies to consider approaches to leading an academic program, a co-curricular program, and looking not only at particular moments (such as a term, semester, or year), but with a longer view as well extending multiple years.

My doctoral degree is in language, equity, and educational policy. It was within the coursework here that created the opportunity for us to examine our unique mentorships, or liberationships as we have come to name them, through developing the liberatory mentorship for women of color model (McAloney & Long, 2019). The doctoral program deepened my understanding of educational inequity within colleges and universities as well as within education as a whole in the United States.

> It is during this experience that I had to consider what I would have to do in order to make it as an academic.
> It was here that I was able to continue considering what resistance within the academy looked like for me.
> It was here that I began my journey to my natural hair and learn to be more comfortable in my own skin and physical appearance largely and within the academy.
> It was because of these liberationships that I could fully bring myself to work.
> It is here that confirmed that this work of liberationships is necessary for my survival and ability to thrive.

Jenesis Rose Long, EdM

My first experience with mentorship taught me that I needed to be different. I was advised to dress differently even though it would make my curvier body uncomfortable, to put more effort into doing my hair so my natural curls didn't look so frizzy, and to do my makeup so the darker pigmentation around my eyes didn't make me look so tired. I was told how to talk, what I should be interested in, and often felt out of place. The core lesson I learned from those years of mentorship was that I was "wrong" and I needed to look different, talk differently, and be different. I left those years of experiences assuming that I would encounter a similar treatment whenever I was being mentored by someone in the future, so I resigned myself to being malleable in order to fit in. I truly believed that in order to achieve my academic or professional goals, I would have to become a different person that someone else shaped, until I met Kim.

A few years after this initial mentorship experience, I transferred to Oregon State University (OSU) to complete my honors Bachelor of Science degree in psychology. As a transfer student, I had just two short years to explore and establish my career goals post-grad. To do this, I pursued student jobs on campus within one of the areas I was interested in, student affairs. I applied to be an academic coach within the Academic Success Center and unfortunately was unable to interview for the position because the funding was cut for their additional staff. When the center's director informed me of that change, she also referred me to meet with Kim McAloney to see about joining the NASPA Undergraduate Fellows Program (NUFP) that is designed to help students from underrepresented backgrounds explore the field of student affairs (NUFP, 2021). When I first met Kim, she explained the program's purpose and structure, and after spending time getting to know me and my interests, she invited me to join. I knew immediately that I wanted to sign up because it would be a great opportunity for me to decide if pursuing a career in student affairs was the right fit for me or not. She then had me review the biographies of the different student affairs professionals that I could ask to serve as my mentor for the program, one of whom was her. Given that our initial conversation flowed so easily and we had many similar identities that influenced how we experienced higher education and careers, I asked if she'd be open to serving as my NUFP mentor. Kim agreed and we applied for the program together after a few more meetings where we clarified my goals. Our application was accepted, and thus began our mentorship relationship.

Participating in the NUFP program with Kim as my mentor allowed me to learn about the field of student affairs, connect with other professionals that Kim had connections with, meet other students with similar identities and interests, and attend a regional NASPA conference. Furthermore, my participation in the NUFP program led to an internship in the Dean of Student Life Office at OSU, a job as an office assistant in the psychology advising office, and was the topic of my undergraduate honors thesis. For my thesis, I wanted to document the impact that mentors had on NUFP students to support improvement of mentorship programs and relationships of underrepresented undergraduate students, since I had received so much personal and professional value.

My original goal of exploring and establishing my career goals was accomplished, and I decided to pursue further studies in higher education administration programs. I applied for the college student services administration (CSSA) program at OSU, along with two other graduate programs for student affairs professionals. While I was accepted to all three, OSU provided the greatest financial incentive for me to achieve professional experience alongside my academic program through the graduate teaching assistantship position I was offered in the University Exploratory Student Program. In this role I served as an academic advisor to exploratory students, as well as a teaching assistant for a career decision-making course, which aligned well with my career goals at the time of becoming an academic advisor.

As I wrapped up my undergraduate degree, I recall reflecting on how my mentorship relationship with Kim was beginning to grow and shift. After 2 years of a formal, structured mentorship relationship, our relationship was now shifting to a new dynamic as I began graduate school. I noticed this because we were starting to engage with each other in new ways, such as broadening our scope of conversation to include things like hair products, relationships, and personal finances. Beyond noticing these differences and feeling grateful for the new ways we were engaging with each other, we also named that this shift was happening. We discussed how my being a graduate student meant I would no longer be an active NUFP fellow, and discussed how we wanted to stay connected to one another through my transition into graduate school.

Part of the CSSA degree requirements is to complete internships that expose you to different areas of the field of student affairs so you gain multiple perspectives of the profession. Through my connection with Kim, I completed an internship in the Educational Opportunities Program (EOP) where I met with multiple academic counselors to learn more about what it means to be an academic counselor so that I could compare it to my experience as an academic advisor, and see how EOP meets their mission of supports the academic, personal, and professional development of students who have traditionally been denied equal access to higher education (Educational Opportunities Program, 2021). Through this internship opportunity, I again saw the value of being mentored by someone you have shared identities with when navigating higher education. This internship, that Kim helped to facilitate, helped me to see that my beliefs about best practices for supporting students aligned more closely with academic counseling than academic advising. The CSSA master's degree program I was in also required students to coordinate a committee of advisors to serve as the reviewers of their portfolio of work and to support their professional development journey. Given my history with Kim, I asked her to serve on my portfolio committee, and she generously agreed. Along with working on developing my academic path and career goals, Kim also helped me see ways that the lessons I was learning and experiences I was gaining could be shared with a larger audience outside of OSU by presenting at conferences. While it took me a while to feel comfortable presenting at conferences, ultimately, it was with Kim's support that I first shared my work with professional associations outside of my university.

Having space within our liberationship to gain self-knowledge of my interests, skills, and goals was critical to guiding me towards my first professional job out of my masters degree as an academic counselor for a grant-funded program that supported first-generation and Pell-eligible college students in a program called "MAAPS" at OSU. As a new student affairs professional, I had much to learn about myself and the world of work. As I navigated questions about my finances, relationships at work and at home, as well as my career path, Kim was there to hold space for me to reflect on my experiences. Unfortunately, the grant funding ended for the program

I was working for, and once they shared their plan to sunset our program, effectively laying us off, I knew it was time to explore my career goals again. Thankfully, I had been growing alongside Kim throughout those years, so she was able to offer support when I shared that I wanted to start my own coaching business as an online entrepreneur.

Mentorship and the Development of Liberationships

Throughout many job and career changes, Kim and my liberationship has persisted and supported each of our growth and development. Because we both had researched mentorship in prior opportunities, we wanted to continue exploring the area together. Ways that I have continued to work with mentorship professionally include through Oregon State University's FIRST! Program that supported first-generation college students to find a mentor, and through the NACADA: The Global Community for Academic Advising by serving as the Region 8 communications coordinator and co-developing their regional mentorship program. Kim continued work with mentorship professionally through Oregon State University's FIRST! program that supported first-generation college students to find a mentor, serving as the NASPA Region V NUFP coordinator, serving as the NUFP, graduate student, and new professional liaison for NASPA's Multiracial and Transracial Adoptee Knowledge Community (now known as the Transracial Adoptee and Multiracial Knowledge Community), and serving as the NUFP, graduate student, and new professional liaison for NASPA's Socioeconomic and Class Issues in Higher Education Knowledge Community, continuing to mentor through supervision of undergraduate and graduate students, OSU Project Social Justice and PROMISE programs, as a CSSA committee member and mentoring graduate students through the institutional review board process, as a Newman Civic Fellowship mentor, OSU's college assistance migrant program scholar intern program, OSU's undergraduate research, scholarship, and arts program, OSU's multiracial Aikido, finally, in mentoring a number of undergraduate and graduate students through the conference proposal and presentation process.

Additional ways we have deepened our understanding of mentorship, the liberatory mentorship for women of color model (McAloney & Long, 2019), and liberationships have included presenting about the model to the following professional associations: Race and Pedagogy Institute, NASPA's Western Regional Conference and Annual conferences, OWHE educational webinar series, OWHE annual conference, Oregon State University Human Resource's FYI Fridays learning series. Furthermore, we have written about the liberatory mentorship for women of color model (McAloney &

Long, 2019) in the following ways: a blog post for OWHE's online resources, four peer-reviewed journal articles for The Mentorship Institute on the model and how it has been applied to our approach to leading a research lab with graduate students as well as shaping our supervision styles, a book chapter in *Teaching and Learning for Social Justice and Equity in Education*, and Kim wrote about the model in her dissertation.

While we have always known the value of our relationship that started as mentorship, we began to recognize there were certain ways about how we engaged with one another that felt unique to our other mentorship relationships and wanted to research its unique factors. This book will showcase the value of Liberationships: Critical Mentorship in Practice.

2

Introduction to Liberatory Mentorship for Women of Color

Do you ever have experiences that just align? That was our experience in the development of this model. We met regularly with the third member of our Liberationship trifecta, Janet Nishihara, as a way to continue to be in relationship and continue to support one another in our similar work as colleagues once our other relationship dynamics of mentor-mentee or supervisor-supervisee had passed. While reflecting during one of those meetings, we discussed that there was something cool, different, and unique about our mentorship relationships. The term mentorship felt unsettling for us and like it didn't fully describe our relationship so we wanted to explore this further and examine the dynamic components of our relationship. One of us suggested exploring that more one day.

The opportunity to explore the unique aspects we had noticed about our relationships presented itself during Kim's doctoral program. For an ethnography course, Kim needed to engage in a research project and thought of the conversation where we all expressed interest in exploring what made our relationship unique between the three of us. The faculty member leading Kim's research course was supportive, and Jenesis and Janet agreed to participate in the project. Their support allowed us to engage in a duoethnography looking at our relationships, our mentorship, and the sort of community and culture we have developed between the three of us. This duoethnography researched three multigenerational relationships spanning 19 years of relationship of three women of color to provide more language to the unique, transformational, and liberatory aspects of these relationships. Through approaching mentorship with critical pedagogies such as engaged pedagogy (hooks, 1998) and *sentipensante* pedagogy (Rendón, 2009), these relationships have developed into spaces of transformative learning, liberation, and as sites as resistance to the systemic power and inequities at a historically White institution that we call Liberationships. Again, liberationships are mutually beneficial relationships that empower all parties to reach their personally-defined goals while addressing systemic barriers. It is these Liberationships that allow us to bring our whole selves to work, engage in meaningful relationships, and sustain ourselves as women of color in higher education. We hope that the theoretical model of *Liberatory Mentorship for Women of Color* can be used to describe such relationships that currently exist, and inspire new relationships to enhance their approach. We encourage readers to consider who, how, and why you engage in mentorship, particularly if you are considering deeper relationships for the purpose of transformation.

Methodology

Our duoethnography study (Sawyer & Norris, 2013) was conducted with three women of color who work at Predominantly White Institutions (PWI) and have been in mentorship relationships for over 19 years combined. Five video-recorded, semi-structured interviews were conducted (Schensul & LeCompte, 2012). We engaged in four 90-minute long sessions using the above research questions as our guide. We began each of these four conversations with reflections on the particular topic for the day and also ended our conversations with reflection specifically about how our thinking shifted from the beginning of our conversation to the end of the conversation. During our fifth and final session together, we looked back at the beginning and end reflections from each of the four previous conversations allowing ourselves to do a meta-analysis of the ways in which our reflective conversations about our relationships helped to shift, change, and hone our thinking. Audio recordings from each session were transcribed and then coded through thematic coding (Gall, Gall, & Borg, 2007).

Introduction to Liberatory Mentorship for Women of Color • **13**

The research questions for Kim's duoethnography study, which we used to guide our discussions were: What is unique about our relationships that began as student-faculty and are now colleague-colleague? What components of our relationship are mentorship and what components are different from mentorship? How do we describe the shifting dynamics/positions within our relationships?

Results

From the qualitative data collected, we developed the transformational mentorship for women of color model (Figure 2.1) to describe several aspects of our relationships and how they work together to create our unique experience.

Overview

The circles on the right side of Figure 2.1 serve as a key to understand the multiple layers of the model. We consider the model to be 3D and we see the model as fully connected and interconnecting. Starting with the gray layer on the bottom is the "who" section, which incorporates three critical factors about who we are that made it possible for us to show up and engage

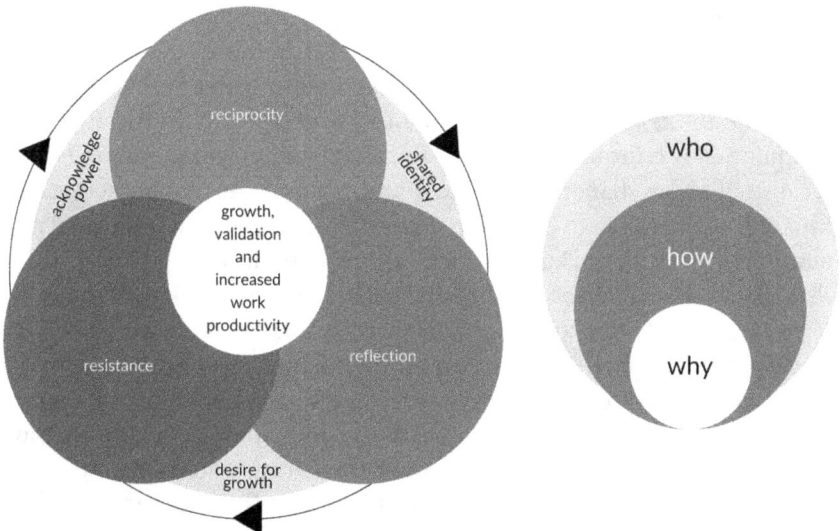

Figure 2.1   The liberatory mentorship for women of color model (McAloney & Long, 2018)

14 ▪ *Liberationships*

with each other in similar ways. Moving up a layer is the darker "how" section, which documents how we engaged with one another so that we could achieve the outcomes documented in the final layer. The top layer of "why" shows the three primary outcomes we identified were only made possible because of the foundational layers of who we are and how we engaged with one another. The outer circle of the model with arrows point out the cyclical nature of our Liberationships that is always changing and growing. The following sections detail each part of the model:

Who

The bottom layer is a gray color and stands for the who section—who are you? This layer of the model are the three most important personal attributes we identified that made it possible for our relationships to be so powerful. Without these three pieces being in place, we may not have been able to engage in the same ways or achieve the same outcomes. Those three areas are (a)

Acknowledge Power

The first personal attribute we identified as helping facilitate our Liberationships is an acknowledgement of power. The ability and willingness to acknowledge power and systems of power, privilege, and oppression, that came from having common language, doing common readings, having similar vocabulary to confront the systems that we (three women of color from rural towns) were working in-all of us working at a historically White institution- was critical to our ability to engage in transformation together. Because of these shared experiences and exposure to similar systems of thinking, we were able to engage in conversations about how individual moments intersect with the larger societal and structural context so we can see what is our personal responsibility, and what we cannot change on our own to set larger goals that affect systems of power if/when we are able. This provided us space to analyze our experiences at work and home from a detached space and offer each other grace when we were unable to change or see power systems that were at play, and also embolden us to look for ways our experiences could be valuable to share during system-level work we supported. We identified that we weren't individuals floating in the world but that we are part of larger systems that are always at play. We are able to acknowledge systems of power and oppression and have the language to be able to do so in conversation, but then also together gained the strength to be able to do so because of our other attributes of having shared identities and a desire for growth.

Shared Identities

The second individual attribute we identified as crucial to developing a transformational mentorship relationship is having shared identities. Having shared identities helped us to be able to understand one another's experiences more easily. While not all of our identities overlap, we do have enough core salient identities that we were able to relate really well with one another when sharing about our lives and goals during our time together. Furthermore, having shared identities gave us similar past experiences and worldviews which we could use to help one another understand what we were going through at work and in our home lives.

The most salient social identities the three of us have in common are identifying as women of color, from rural areas, that came from lower income/working class backgrounds, and a whole host of other identities that we discovered over time. It's not necessary that folks have all the same identities, but some core identities that allow you to look through or at your experiences to find commonalities and help one another process those experiences are critical for the outcomes identified in the model.

Desire for Growth

The third and final attribute the three of us identified is a desire for growth. One of our individual values was a commitment to and desire for learning and growing both through reading and learning in classroom-based environments, but also through discussions with one another that took the shape of being reflective and wanting to grow emotionally and intellectually. Within our relationships, this allowed us to grow holistically because we were able to allow each other to be influenced by one another's lived experience and knowledge. This shared attribute about "who" we are showed up for us during times where we were able to say, "I'm trying this and it's not working. Do you have advice for me?" or "I'm trying this new thing but could I be trying more?" and having an influential and supportive voice there from others to say, "Yes, and..." or "Well, maybe you could be stretching this way, instead?" Because we have a shared desire for growth, we were able to show up in our mentorship relationships aware that we don't know all the answers, but are consistently saying, "I'm here and I trust you for input." This shared desire also was exemplified in our overlapping commitment to serving as educators.

How

The next layer of the model is the red, large circles. This layer describes the moments in our relationship where we experienced the most unique way of relating to one another as opposed to our other mentorship experiences. The three significant ways we engaged with each other were: resistance, reciprocity, and reflection. These three approaches to relating to one another provided unique opportunities for support when navigating PWIs and systemic power injustices at work and in our home lives that made it possible for us to sustain our commitment to our work as educators.

Resistance

The first of three ways we relate to one another is resistance. This aspect is situated between "acknowledging power" and a "desire for growth" because without those two personal attributes, we would not be able to engage in resistance with one another during our mentorship conversations. Resistance can be understood as a willingness to witness injustices or inequities and a commitment to growing those systems to make positive change.

In practice, resistence looked like being able to challenge each other's ways of thinking that mirrored oppressive ways of being, or hold space for each other to witness what was going on in a bigger societal context and then try to advocate for and support each other to improve our approach towards more liberatory and freeing ways. An example of this in practice looked like when a senior executive at the university was putting pressure on Jenesis to lead the development of a program to serve first-generation students in a way that would not best serve the highest-need participants. Jenesis knew that she did not want to conform to the leader's pressure, but on her own was unable to identify how to speak back to this person in power in a way that was graceful and clear, while also not getting her fired. Through supportive conversations that centered this resistance, Jenesis was supported to both acknowledge the systems of power at play between her and the executive leader's positionality in the university structure, and support Jenesis to grow her self-advocacy skills by identifying a route to speak her truth and remove herself from the growing pressure of doing what she knew was wrong for the students involved. This allowed Jenesis to experience resistance to her known ways of behaving in a situation like this, ultimately providing her with greater leadership skills, and increased her professional capacity as a better communicator due to learning from the wisdom of her mentorship partners, resulting in a more liberatory way of engaging at work.

An additional part of engaging in resistance is choosing to show up as our whole selves in the PWIs we work. As women of color from low-income backgrounds at PWIs, we often got messages that we needed to conform to the dominant culture and engage in the White supremacist, capitalist system to uphold professionalism standards set within that context. However, when we are in fast-moving meeting spaces with colleagues or students or responding to dozens of emails while a campus crisis is happening, we need to be able to act authentically and trust our intuition to lead our actions. To release the need to uphold the expectations of how we are taught to be and truly be able to bring our whole selves into our work is an act of resistance in the workplace that took support. This resistance was brought out through supportive conversations in our Liberationships because during our time together we encouraged each other to show up as our whole selves, challenges, questions, joys, quirks, natural hair, and everything in between. Therefore, we were practicing how to be comfortable in our own skin, with our own histories, and with our own cultures in the workplace. This in-group experience then led to us being more authentically ourselves when engaging with the larger community of our institution, allowing us to increase our impact.

Reciprocity

Reciprocity is about giving and taking in our relationships and not having the benefits garnered from the dynamic be unidirectional, which is the most common way mentorship is discussed in previous literature. Reciprocity is situated by "acknowledge power" and "shared identity" because it requires looking at your identities that are similar—and different—to see what power structures might be at play between those involved in the relationship, as well as being able to acknowledge what systems of power have created those imbalances to then take action together to dismantle the influences of power on the relationship. Acknowledging systems and dynamics that create an imbalance of power is helpful, but doing something with it is why our relationships became such transformative spaces for growth. For example, Janet was Kim's supervisor for a while. When this professional power dynamic began, they needed to acknowledge this shift in their relationship, while also re-committing to the desire to have a more balanced way of relating to one another during their mentorship conversations. So while during staff meetings and budgeting decisions or professional reviews, Janet did serve as the decider and guide, during mentorship meetings, Janet could serve more as a partner, allowing Kim to trust Janet with more information regarding her feelings and needs.

In most mentorship literature, there's the knower (mentor) and then the learner (mentee) with not much space for the mentor to be learning from the mentee or if there is, it's only sharing specific pieces information rather than a transformative amount of learning, it is not a priority or expectation and it just happens to occur as a one-off dynamic, rather than an integral way for that relationship to function. Reciprocity is recognizing that both mentorship partners have something to give, teach, and share. This approach to mentorship allows the mentor to not need to make all the decisions, and to be able to grow with their mentee. This also can support the mentee's confidence by validating that they have knowledge and wisdom to share with someone further along their future path.

In practice, this most often looked like conversations being a space to share ideas, resources, and offer challenges to one another's thinking, back and forth. Reciprocity can also take place during work meetings where the liberationship partners are both involved. An example of this is when we were all participating in a committee meeting at our university and Kim shared an idea that the facilitator glossed over. Rather than allowing her words to go unnoticed, Jenesis echoed Kim's idea and Janet validated its helpfulness. Together, these incremental shifts in behavior within this committee meeting resisted the historical practice of denying and overlooking women of color's voices in professional spaces. Through reciprocity we can help each other be heard and seen.

Reflection

The third and final integral piece we documented within "how" we related to one another is reflection. Reflection is situated above "desire for growth" and "shared identities" within the model. Being okay with having needs, knowing what you need, and then bringing it to your Liberationship to seek support of reciprocity and shared resistance requires reflection. In our research, we found reflection to be the primary way we spoke to one another during our mentorship conversations. Rather than providing direct suggestions or advice, we shared reflective narratives based on our past to demonstrate our understanding of each other's experience. We found this approach to be helpful because it allowed us to come alongside one another as a partner who "gets it" rather than speaking from an authoritative place. Reflection showed up both as responding to questions about how we are doing and what we are feeling lately, but also in response to each others' sharing.

During mentorship relationships such as ours, it is common to need to ask for support. However, acknowledging that you need support may take some self-awareness that can come about through verbal reflection first. Receiving advice after this type of conversation can lead to being more receptive to it. If someone tries to tell you that you are doing something incorrectly or could improve your methods to achieve your desired outcomes without you having consented to receiving their support by first recognizing you need it and then asking for the other person to share about their similar experiences, it is likely that you will become defensive. Using the approach of offering reflections gave us space to provide insights from our experiences without becoming the authority over how the individual we were speaking ought to act. We were able to provide pathways they may not have yet considered without making decisions for their unique situation. Being willing to be vulnerable and honest and to share the real feelings whether that's, "I'm really nervous for this meeting," or "I was really upset by that comment so-and-so made." Then being able to be with one another in that moment of contemplation, sharing our real feelings, thoughts and questions or validating that we also are unsure of how to act in that type of engagement normalized our struggles.

Reflection also allowed us to acknowledge shifts in our relationships as new dynamics emerged requiring us to adjust and set new boundaries as we moved from student–teacher to supervisor–employee to now colleagues. We were able to pause and reflect together to identify when things needed to change so that we could continue our relationship. We identified that this space to pause and reflect is why our relationships were able to sustain for so long and produce such great impact on our careers and lives—we grew together. Being able to reflect honestly with each other about how we wanted to continue engaging allowed us to continue building strong, honest, and supportive relationships.

Why

Lastly, let's examine why we cultivate Liberationships, or said another way, what we get out of being in Liberationships as active participants of these liberatory relationships. By creating space for reflection, resistance, and reciprocity with people who have shared identities, a commitment to growth, and an ability to acknowledge power, we identified that the three primary outcomes of Liberationships are: growth, validation, and increased work productivity/contribution to community.

All three participants in the research study identified ways we were able to grow only because of the work we did in this intentional relationship with one another. We were able to identify this growth because our relationships starting gave us a clear "starting point" pre-relationship for us to examine where we were in our career and lives and where we got to, thus witnessing how our liberationships impacted our personal and professional growth. Because we were able to engage with one another about our whole lives, not just the work components of our lives, we identified ways that we shifted holistically because of our Liberationships. They helped us hold community care and self-care to protect and prioritize our own personal growth as the priority it is when making important and influential decisions. As higher education professionals, we talk a lot about self-care as a way to sustain our energy for our work, but we have found that most struggle at practicing it during organizational decisions-making processes, particularly as budget cuts have asked us to do more with less (more work, increase in outcomes both with less staff, less professional development, less operating budgets, and less flexibility), resulting in negative outcomes for individuals well-being or ability to prioritize the things that matter to them. As we were able to have clarity on our values through reflective conversations with one another, and be challenged and supported by our liberationship partners, we were able to increase our sense of self and achieve more at work/in our community including earning graduate degrees and publishing scholarly works. This growth being witnessed and talked about by our liberationship partners created a sense of validation, a feeling that as individuals with numerous historically marginalized identities, was surprising and delightful to find. As we grew personally and professionally, so did our liberationship relationships. They continued to deepen, allowing for new growth to show up in how we engaged, our ways of thinking and being, how we approached the world and our work. This also required us to continue improving our ability to know ourselves, each other, and community. As our priorities and values changed over time, so did our needs and boundaries. We prioritized flexibility and understanding one another as we grew. This approach is why we were able to engage with one another for such long time periods, creating an ongoing sense of belonging within our relationships. This is important because the connection with people who allowed us to bring all of who we are into our work made it so we could move toward our goals faster and with more aligned-action. Being able to be validated in our positionalities is necessary for us to stay engaged in work and live in large systems like higher education that were not set up for us to be included, let alone successful within it. This validation was not only of ourselves in our identities, but also our experiences, our reasons for doing the type of work we were engaged in, and how we understood our work, division, institution, and higher work of the field. This validation also supported each of us through navigating the imposter syndrome, bureaucracy within the system, and toxic relationships. We each share similar values and desires for our work as educators and this validation helped support us in continuing to do meaningful work.

This growth and validation lead to increased work productivity because we have these dynamic relationships where we could stack projects together and think critically about our professional and personal goals. We are able to see how we could work together, where else we could be serving, and also manage increasing what we are able to do in a way that sustains us for the long term thanks to our supportive, long-term liberationships. We are able to share with one another that we might be adding another task to our plates and the other can prompt and engage us in a conversation about how this new task fits within the other components of our role and work we are individually and collectively engaging in. This helps us ensure we are being productive in our work but not at the expense of our well-being, creating a more sustainable work/life relationship. An example of this is how we created this model, wrote and published multiple academic book chapters, wrote this book, and continue encouraging one another to try innovative approaches to out and apply for promotions, start our own small businesses, register for conferences, or submit a conference session proposal. These three outcomes make it easy for us to stay committed to engaging in our current liberationships, and seek new ones with similarly aligned individuals.

The final part of the model is a circle with little arrows around the outside, encompassing the who, how, and why sections. This is to highlight that this entire relational system, all of the individual pieces, are ever-changing and continue to shift. The outside circle shows that it's an ever evolving and dynamic model. If we were to create an animated visual of this model, we would show that throughout the arch of a liberationship dynamic, sometimes one piece will be really big, while another is smaller, depending on our needs at the time. Over time, this will continue to shift and look different. We know this because our relationships have lasted decades of time. They've stayed strong, stayed important, and stayed valuable through many different versions of ourselves and different stages in life due to our commitment to one another's growth as well as our own. At one point, we maybe wouldn't have talked about xy and z, but in two years, we started talking about it and so we're always reevaluating if things are working for us and if not, we adjust. Finally, we imagine this model as a 3D structure where all of the components are happening at the same time and are in continual motion to fully capture the dynamic and complex factors that create liberationships. These types of liberatory relationships are ever evolving and dynamic to hold space for the human experience that is equally as nuanced.

How We Named the Model

We would also like to share that the duoethnography research study was conducted on and with the three of us: women of color all working in academic support programs who were first-generation college students from low-income backgrounds and raised in rural communities for some or all of our childhoods. Given such, we titled the model, "Liberatory Mentorship for Women of Color in Higher Education." Our identities as women of color are what we thought was the connector. As we have shared this work locally and nationally via book chapters and conferences, folks have shared with us that this model works for people who identify as male, LGBTQIAASS+, first-generation, and other dynamics of power that exist within their relationships. We have also had the opportunity to supervise graduate students and we encourage them to learn this model with us and invite them to engage in this type of work with us, specifically making our supervision more like mentorship, and we were able to validate that it still works across different identities through those relationships, too. These additional spaces that liberationships can help others has been encouraging to see and motivates us to continue to consider the model's potential impact through writing, thinking, and relationships.

3

Mentorship Is More Than Meets the Eye

In this chapter, we will discuss our vision and mentorship goals, how we benefited from mentorship, how we hope and recommend what mentorship looks like, and how mentorship impacts and grows the individuals involved. This chapter begins to discuss why mentorship matters personally and systemically to those who are marginalized and that attend and/or work within higher education.

As detailed in the previous chapter, we were paired up in a mentorship relationship. Through our formal mentorship and informal mentorship relationship's years, we recognized that our experiences were something deeper. They were more fulfilling and empowering than what we had experienced through other mentorship experiences. Our mentorship relationship became an essential part of sustaining and furthering our work. We discussed this in a meeting with Janet. A few months later, we were able to engage in the research that led to the development of the liberatory mentorship for women of color (McAloney & Long, 2019). As we engaged in the research and exploration of these relationships, we realized through reviewing mentorship literature that our relationships were something different and deeper. We were in mentorship relationships, but our experience was more than mentorship, hence the discussion of our mentorship as being more than meets the eye.

Coming Into Our Racial Selves

For the two of us, Jenesis and Kim, specifically, at the beginning of our mentorship relationship, we were both exploring our identities as multiracial/biracial. After taking the Black Identity course with Larry, Kim was attending professional conferences and meeting other student affairs professionals who had a shared identity of being multi- and biracial.

I, Kim, remember being in the room with other multiracial folks who had an interest in building a space for ourselves as part of NASPA and I remember having tears in my eyes as I'd never felt as whole or as seen as I was in that room with folks who deeply understood me and my experiences. This moment of being in a room where we all shared an aspect of our racial identity as opposed to always being on the margins of monoracial spaces was powerful.

For Jenesis, it was in our conversations and mentorship space that she recognized she was not White. She shares,

> I didn't know I wasn't White until we started talking and then it clicked like, I was called the Brown girl and Brownie, and was clearly marked as other in experiences that I had, but it didn't really click for me then.

Kim was at the beginning of her professional career and Jenesis was considering her options post-undergrad while together we were exploring what it meant to be multiracial woman of color. That thread along with our racial exploration and identity development pushed us beyond the bounds of mentorship. Because of this racial third space that our lived experience presented to us, we were able to move from mentorship into this third space of mentorship, later being named liberationships, so naturally. It was in our conversations and liberationships with Janet who really helped us understand, situate, and make intentional decisions on how we wanted to show up together, individually, and in our work (which later we identified as being through: reflection, reciprocity, resistance).

Identity work is so necessary for liberationships and why mentorship without identity work can feel shallow. The latter is like you're not looking at who you are in those spaces in which you are engaging in mentorship both for the mentorship relationships itself, but also the reasons behind engaging in the mentorship in the first place. For us, we could learn how to be a student affairs and higher education practitioner but what about the way we showed up as our minoritized (and privileged) selves in spaces as student affairs and higher education practitioners? What about the way people view us because of how we show up in all of our identities as student affairs and higher education practitioners?

One of our salient identities is race. We cannot imagine not being able to articulate or help one another identify and articulate what is happening to us as well as the feelings we are feeling with those experiences of marginalization and violence. This includes even the most common experiences in higher education like going to a conference or applying for graduate school. Without the additional context of who we are in those spaces and how we are perceived, it is like we were speaking a different language or like we did not have the sound turned on while watching a movie. Without these explicit identity discussions, we missed a whole other layer of input and stimuli that is happening and that we just didn't know enough about it to interpret it. Through our conversations we are able to gain understanding of the systems of oppression that were impacting our experiences that helped us see why we have these feelings. Our identity-based liberationship conversations also help us understand why it is hard to sometimes answer other's questions, particularly those that create a distance and an othering effect. And othering is the antithesis of belonging, right?

It's hard to feel belonging in a space where you do not know or understand why you don't belong in that space or that the space was designed for you to not belong within it. Education was not designed for us, as women of color, to be successful. Our liberationships supported one another to figure out that we *could* belong in these spaces, in higher education. In addition to the recognition that we could belong within the space, it was within our liberationships that we were able to understand, work through, and support one another in having the power to show up the way we desire to within the space of higher education. It was and is because of our shared identities that we could support one another within this space of belonging and resistance. What would we have done without someone to reflect, debrief and contextualize why things feel the way they feel, and develop a strong sense of who we are and could be in higher education?!

As part of this understanding of experiences and finding belonging comes the importance of naming. While in college as students, we learn a lot of vocabulary before we can advance through coursework from lower division credit to upper division credits. We also must understand the vocabulary of our desired field if we are to consider graduate school. Within liberationships, it's important to be able to engage with social justice concepts (being able to acknowledge) and have the vocabulary around systems of power and privilege. Being aware of these concepts allow for being able to name the differences in power we see happening to others or experience ourselves.

Within our relationships, we share about our identities, reflect on our experiences, and support one another as we name the systems of oppression influencing us and our experiences. Being able to name these racialized and gendered feelings and experiences help us to be able to identify and name how we want to choose to respond in situations and how we want to engage as leaders. It is one thing to learn from a textbook and another to name experiences or concepts in real life while we are experiencing it.

Within graduate school, students often question how information and concepts will be used asking: "How do we apply a particular theory in its series?"; "What will I do with students to help them progress through this theoretical model?"; "What will I say?"; "How will I coach students through certain situations?"; "What will I teach students?" Jenesis shared that even though she never took an ethnic studies or social justice course during her undergraduate experience, it was our liberationship that she began graduate school so much farther ahead because of what she learned through our discussions of our experiences. Jenesis shares that it was the readings Kim shared, the naming of experiences, and "holding space and talking all that [Kim] knew and applying it to my situations with me to be like, 'that's called this' or 'did you feel like that? Oh, well, that's because of this, that could be happening.'" This in the moment support of navigational capital (Yosso, 2005) and being able to help Jenesis recognize what was happening to her helped her normalize her experiences as a woman of color in higher education. This also led to helping her consider ways she could engage more fully in these experiences and higher education as a whole. This work didn't seem like the easing mentorship found in women of color literature (McAloney, 2021). Often, this can be an assumed benefit of mentorship, but teaching people how to engage in understanding and strategy around navigating with their social identities and actually do this kind of support and engagement is lacking in literature. This is so much more than teaching technical skills or higher level "here's the step-by-step" of how to engage.

This brings us back to those graduate students' questions. Let's discuss the "Okay, I learned this theoretical series but what does it look like in practice?" question. The application of theory and knowledge is personalized support in the moment with others and in this case, people call it mentorship. The space to do this, because there is this assumed closeness and ability to do this personalized naming and support, but that skill development is severely lacking from most people's mentorship skill set. Mentors just think that they can focus on the more tangible things, but not the intangible thoughts, feelings, and reflections their mentees might be experiencing. Without being able to hold space for the deep seeded work connected to social identities and systems of power and oppression our mentees only can grow so far.

There are not a lot of resources on how to be a mentor particularly in ways that center identity. Sometimes it feels easier to see something in someone else's life and name it than examining that same experience in one's own life. As Kim was supporting Jenesis in naming her experiences and feelings, Kim was also reflecting on her own experiences. The shared identity of being multiracial and exploring that together, allowed for both of us to engage in reflection, reciprocity, and resistance.

The Evolution of Mentorships Into Liberationships

So much literature on mentorship discusses mentorship as one directional. But as Kim was going through, maybe just ahead of Jenesis, really examining what does it mean to be a racialized being and to be a multi-racialized being. Our mentorship conversations allowed Kim to be able to also reflect and learn from the conversations that she could consider and apply in her own life and experiences.

The NUFP program has two learning outcomes around examining power and privilege which was able to impact both of our experiences within the program and our subsequent careers. Through NUFP and her major, Kim, an ethnic studies major in undergrad, she had conversations about power, privilege, and oppression all the time both in and out of the classroom. Graduate school, however, was a starkly different experience. While Kim found social justice conversations with mentors, supervisors, and cohort mates, the dialogues were minimal if they showed up at all in the graduate classroom. As we began our mentorship, Kim was a professional in her first professional role and examining her multiraciality. These experiences and conversations with Jenesis were key to Kim's own growth and development at this time as well. They gave her deep, justice-related conversations she was used to (through her undergraduate experiences in her major and the NUFP program), but was missing during graduate school and largely as a professional. This ability of reciprocity or mutual sharing and learning calls upon Freire's (1970) teacher–student and student–teacher relationship as well as bell hooks' (1998) engaged pedagogy where the faculty member and students co-create a learning community together through the facilitation of community by the faculty member. Openness to the topics and conversations with Jenesis, rather than dismissing, allowed for a realness and openness that both of us were able to lean into.

The modeling of this type of mentorship and liberationship came from Kim's liberationship with Janet. Janet showed that Kim might have insight or something to offer and contribute to Janet's thinking and processing as she engages in vulnerability with Kim as a new professional. They also had taught together for a couple years as of this point in time and seeing her example of being open to try Kim's innovative ideas and projects, and Janet sharing and talking out her thinking and processing, including sometimes things she was wrestling with, made a space where Kim felt she could ask any question—that they could discuss any topic which then Kim reflected in facilitating her mentorship with Jenesis. It was these moments and this work that helped us shift from the ways in which Eurocentric mentorship, with a clear hierarchy and limitations on professional selves, to liberationships in which as a community, we could build a container of reciprocity; one of which allowed us to bring our full selves, both professional *and* personal, to the space.

One way to name what we just described is humility. This personality attribute of humility is an identity of a true lifelong learner that Janet and Kim both exampled. This humility holds that anyone you're engaging with has the capacity to teach you something and to positively influence you. This is something that Jenesis' late stepdad taught her. While we are unsure of the actual quote, what she remembers and took away from that lesson was that everyone you know knows something better than anyone else you know and your job is to figure out what that is and to learn about it from them. Isn't this wild in the best way? It's exciting to hold one another's humanity and regard each person as a knower of knowledge with the ability to teach you something. For us, this is exciting! This cultural humility and curiosity is a powerful way to approach relationships.

Both Jenesis and Kim spent a lot of time as children feeling alone, misunderstood, and intentionally left out as their families moved a lot. Neither were able to build a deep community given the short time of being in any one space. It really bothered Jenesis that people couldn't and wouldn't open up to deep relationships faster because she knew she was going to move in a year. Her approach was, can't we just become best friends tomorrow? She and Kim desired friendship and deep community, but other people needed a longer time to build connection and trust. We believe this came from a place of not believing that everyone has inherent value. It's the curiosity from the lesson above that speaks to us in this conversation. If you know that every person you're interacting with has value, you will care about them from the beginning, including caring about their ideas. This reminds us of Kim's experience working with Janet since her time in undergrad. As we worked together in the bridge program, teaching first year engagement courses, Kim always had these different ideas and ways of doing things that could easily have been written off. Had Janet and Kim been engaging in a hierarchical mentorship that established Janet as the only authority or holding all of the knowledge, Kim never would have found her love of teaching or approach her work with the creativity that she does today. This space to contribute along with Janet supported both of theirs, and subsequently the students they taught and worked with learning and connection. A different mentor could have taken Kim's ideas as their own and capitalized on them for their own personal advancement, but Janet facilitated the liberationship that allowed both of us to flourish in our own ways through the support of our shared identities and connections that are the foundation of our relationship. As we have this shared desire for growth and humility to learn from one another, we both were able to grow. This belief in each person having something to teach another is an act of resistance within the academy. Higher education is the foundation of elitism in the United States and building up minoritized undergraduates through liberationships is starkly against this elitism. This openness, this humility and deep engagement with one another's humanness requires examples that knowledge comes in various ways and that as people, we are not empty vessels as students.

This piece about the institution being elitist directly ties to the foundation of racial capitalism in the United States. These concepts and structures at their core, literally take away people's humaneness in order to exploit them for the gain of the White elite ruling class. In considering these foundations, this humility is not only an act of resistance to the way in which knowledge is considered, but is also a link in connecting people in a deeply, genuine human sort of way. Recognizing creates a healing space where we all can flourish. This leadership quality was taught to us by Larry, Janet, and Mamta. Each of them created and held space for others' humanity. This helped us consider how we could grow into our own leadership styles that became necessary for us to do the work that we want to do in supporting others. These three examples and elders, helped us understand that there were multiple ways of leading, multiple ways of learning, multiple epistemologies to bring our work, multiple pedagogies that inform the practice of our work, and that we could build deep, meaningful liberationships beyond the hierarchy of mentorship.

As a mentee, Jenesis hoped that she created a space for Kim to bring her whole self to conversations and the relationship which again is how we got here. hooks (1998) posits that both the instructor and the students have to agree to enter in engaged pedagogy. In a similar manner, this is what Jenesis and Kim were able to do. It was then in this liberation space that allowed Jenesis to resist during her honors thesis in terms of topic, in terms of research methodology, and in approach to writing. She chose to examine mentorship as her thesis topic. Jenesis engaged in a qualitative study even though Psychology is so often quantitative. She chose to write through scholarly personal narrative as opposed to the elitist language of the academy. While others may have thought her work was not scholarly, it was her liberationship with Kim and relationship with Larry, and others connected to NUFP, that gave her the confidence to intentionally make decisions to resist the elitist structures of the academy including that of the Honors College.

Jenesis, in the writing of this book, recounted Larry, who was the chair of her honors undergraduate thesis committee, expressed a few times that he thought Jenesis was brilliant. Jenesis navigated through her imposter syndrome through the support of Kim. The pushback on the elitism of higher education that Jenesis was experiencing around her honors thesis was difficult for her to navigate with pressures coming from the Honors College and others. It was through her work with Kim and the data from her thesis topic examining NUFP mentorship relationships and what NUFP students got out of the experience that she realized there could be radical change in a student's experience through mentorship. She realized that our role as student affairs professionals can truly be a change agent. So often, mentorship is about the mentor creating versions of themselves versus engaging in liberationships which are really centered on helping people become their best selves and more expressed versions of themselves. Kim was an active part of giving feedback to Jenesis throughout the thesis process providing space to process after Jenesis' meetings with Larry or with the Honors College. While others shared with Jenesis that her work was "not real research" and her intimidation of the Vice Provost of Student Affairs Larry Roper serving as her chair, Kim was a safe, go-between for processing and supporting Jenesis to make the decisions she wanted to make and to stand firm in them. It was because of this intentional support that Jenesis knew she was doing important and valid work, just as Kim was doing for her.

In a similar manner, Kim's master's thesis committee included Larry, Mamta, and Janet. As already discussed, Kim's positionality (Kim's social identities and lived experiences and the work or lack thereof she had done around social identities power and privilege at that time) in relationships with the three of them (read: feelings of intimidation of and the authority of Larry and Mamta's actual work positions) led her to gravitate to Janet for questions and to talk things out. Kim felt she needed someone on her committee who she could ask those first-generation-college-student questions to without the positional pressure.

As Kim experienced these different leadership models from Janet, Larry, and Mamta that held these deep seated values that she also felt, Kim was able to consider her leadership epistemology and pedagogy. Creating a space for her to bring her full self and having critical pedagogies to tie her work to, Kim could embed liberatory praxis. Though all three of these mentors supported Kim in the healing work around the internalized oppressions that impacted her social identities and opened up her dual consciousness, it was the liberationship with Janet, and Jenesis that have allowed her to talk out and reflect on what resistance within the academy looks like to her specifically. Thankfully her liberationship with Janet helps give her the tools and ongoing support to do this.

Supervision

When Jenesis recounts her supervision experiences and relationships with multiple supervisors in and out of higher education, she recognizes not having shared identities with any of them, particularly around race or class. She also always assumed a class difference as each of these supervisors made more money than she so inherently they had more value. She remembers vividly a look of shock of one assigned supervisor commenting that she had straightened her hair. The comment was something that included like, "Oh, your hair is different. What happened?" and she responded with the fact that she had straightened it. This supervisor asked why she had done this, leaving her in the moment asking whether the supervisor was calling her out with negative intentions. She wondered if her hair looked bad or if this supervisor liked her natural curls. While there could have been a different way for the supervisor to express this sentiment, Jenesis took in that her supervisor was criticizing her look that day. Now every time Jenesis straightens her hair, she thinks about this moment. We have identified that a toxic behavior of a mentor is sharing that their mentee can talk with them about anything, but then the mentor never makes space for the mentee to share. Again, so often the mentor wants to have their mentees almost as minions who then emulate that mentor in how they walk and talk. This, however, is not developing a real relationship nor allowing the mentee to be who they are. In the scenario with the supervisor and Jenesis' hair, she had no context for why her supervisor was bringing up her different hair style that day. She experienced her boss provide criticism without consent as they had never talked about hair in any other space within their relationship to that point.

Not only were Jenesis and Kim able to talk about race and their shared experience as multiracial individuals, but we were also able to talk about socioeconomic status, class, money, and money issues. We built a relationship that allowed us to engage in these conversations that otherwise it feels so unsafe to share. We had to make meaning around our ever changing relationships with money and one another and name what we could and could not talk about. This meant that we had a conversation that allowed us to feel more comfortable in actually engaging in those conversations that are the "You can talk about anything" topics. A metaphor here is if someone started taking their shirt off with you, you might question why in the world they were doing that. But if you had talked about the fact they wanted to and felt comfortable to take off their shirt, and had consent from you that it was okay, it would make sense. This naming and consent is so important.

We created the liberatory mentorship for women of color model because we couldn't find any literature that helped explain our experience. This naming and ideas of consent allowed for a natural deepening of our mentorship relationship. This is true partially because Jenesis had experiences where consent was taken away from her as a child. The multiple abuse strategies that created space for her sexual abuser provides the background in which naming and consent are so important. As we talked about our families, about support we were getting or not, as we shared about times we felt devalued due to the lack of consent allowed for the naming in our relationship, in our liberationship about what we could talk about what we could not talk about was incredibly important. This was a polar opposite against the disrespect and devaluing of our choices or lack of choices that we had as children. Again this comes back to people valuing other people as human beings and respecting the authority that comes with that. This includes an understanding that the person you are engaging with is different than you and might engage differently than you, but that you are willing to embark on the journey together. Another analogy that we can that might make more sense is that if we were to make food and walk up to someone and hand them the food and make them eat it. We don't know if they actually like the food we prepared or not. We don't know if they are allergic to any of the ingredients we used within the dish. This idea of the other person needing to consent to taking and eating the food is so critical to honoring that person as a human who has choices and the ability to consent on what they put into their bodies. This consent piece also documents and recognizes someone else's boundaries and recognizes that those boundaries exist.

One thing this topic of consent made us think about is enmeshment. Enmeshment is an over-investment in a relationship in which one person has with another. They assume that the person in the enmeshed relationship with them has the same thoughts, needs, drives, and preferences as they do. Enmeshment is the opposite of consent. It is a relationship in which you as an individual have nothing that is yours as an individual. If you then act out of character, the other person indicates that you're wrong or bad and you'll be punished. An example of this could be someone giving another person they are enmeshed with a cookie. If the person who is being presented the cookie says that they're not hungry, the person offering the cookie then asks, "how could you not be hungry?" and continues asking, "Why aren't you hungry? Don't you like my cooking?" Enmeshment allows for no space between the two people for any types of differences.

Both Jenesis and Kim experienced enmeshment in our past. Coming to these liberationships was literally liberating. We found that we could be in healthy, close relationships with another person who can help us learn and grow. We were able to bring our full, real selves to our liberationships and know that we would be cared for within the relationship. We could ask each other questions. We could say no. We could share that something was not right and disagree comfortably, safely. This space was a liberated space that helped us to consider what relationships and being able to engage as our full selves could be. Jenesis shares that as a child she didn't feel safe and she learned that it was safer to not express her true thoughts and feelings because they were always wrong. Kim has felt a similar way in areas of her life as well and had become guarded. And yet, our liberationships let us be our full selves and express our own individuality. Liberationships, differently than mentorship, are designed to help you flourish as your own self, to contribute in your own way to validate who you are, to feel yourself grow, into a newer, more expressed version of yourself versus conforming to be more like someone else. We recognize that the ability to have liberationships and to engage in these relationships is a luxury and a privilege that we've both been granted because of our educational attainment. These systems of oppression tell us that we're not good enough and that we're not human enough. While we recognize that our moms and families were doing their best to help us be like them and survive, this enmeshment and survival of our White mothers was not our path. While it can be easy to get caught up in similar behavior to others, with liberationships, we have been able to transform ourselves; to grow, to learn, to be the people that we want to be in the world.

A critique we have about the institution is that the barrier should be lowered; no one no one should struggle to be a part of an institution of higher education. The system of higher education has become a business that is disguised as not a business. Institutions of higher ed are businesses operating for profit. This helps us contextualize and make sense why folks don't feel comfortable or don't feel part of the organization. It's a system of racial capitalism in the clothing of nonprofit goodwill. There are small pockets of individuals who are changing educational systems within their purview. We have been able to survive this educational space for so long or have decided to leave the system to become entrepreneurs making meaning of our education and experiences in different ways and not be a part of the confused and shrouded system anymore. Audre Lorde shares that one cannot tear down the master's house with the master's tools. Our liberationships have helped us survive and find thrivance where and when we could while we were, or are, a part of the system.

In conclusion, this chapter has taken us on a deeply personal and introspective journey into the transformative power of mentorship. Through the lens of our own experiences, we have explored the complexities of mentorship relationships that go beyond the surface and delve into the depths of identity, belonging, and social justice. Our liberationship, rooted in shared racial identities and a commitment to growth and reflection, have allowed us to navigate the challenges and nuances of higher education with newfound understanding and resilience.

Through our mentorship and liberationship conversations, we have discovered the importance of naming and critically examining the systems of power and privilege that shape our experiences. It is through these conversations that we have been able to find validation, articulate our feelings, and develop a sense of agency within the spaces of higher education. We have realized that liberationships are not just about technical skills or following prescribed steps; it is about engaging in personalized support, deep reflection, and the facilitation of meaningful connections.

This chapter has emphasized the need for mentorship programs that center identity and incorporate liberatory practices. It has highlighted the significance of cultural humility, open dialogue, and inclusive evaluation measures in fostering transformative mentorship relationships. We have advocated for mentorship programs that prioritize mutual growth, reflection, reciprocity, and resistance, enabling mentees to have input and choice in the matching process.

In sharing our journey, we hope to inspire others to embrace liberatory mentorship and recognize the profound impact it can have on personal and professional development. We invite mentors and mentees to engage in transformative action, challenge systemic barriers, and foster inclusive and empowering relationships. Let us create a mentorship landscape that embraces the complexities of identity, acknowledges power dynamics, and fosters a sense of belonging for all individuals within higher education.

As we conclude this chapter, we are reminded of the words of Freire (1970) and hooks (1998), highlighting the co-creation of learning communities and the importance of engaged pedagogy. We encourage mentors and mentees to embark on this journey together, engaging in reflective conversations, mutual sharing, and continuous learning. By embracing liberatory mentorship, we can pave the way for a more just and equitable higher education landscape, where every individual can thrive and contribute their unique perspectives and talents.

Now that we've had a chance to share with you a little bit more about our views on mentorship systems, how we have benefited from mentorship, what we hope and recommend mentorship could look like, and how it impacts individuals, we transition into the rest of the book. These next couple chapters will talk about the history of higher educational institutions and discuss the ways in which women of color, particularly, were left out providing context to why women of color are and often feel as outsiders in the institution. We will also talk about mentorship and mentorship literature particularly around women of color mentorship.

4

Literature on Mentorship

In order to gain a comprehensive understanding of mentorship and its significance within communities of color in higher education, it is essential to examine the existing literature. By delving into previous research, we can identify the individuals who have been studied, explore different types of mentorship that have been discussed, and situate our own discourse within this scholarly landscape. This chapter serves as an introductory overview of the literature on mentorship in higher education, particularly focusing on women of color. Additionally, we will provide a brief summary of our critical pedagogical approach to mentorship, which has led us to embrace the concept of liberationships.

Mentorship Among Women of Color

As we examined literature about women of color mentorship within higher education, we found a few themes. These themes include: (a) women of color ways of knowing; (b) finding a community women feel personally and professionally connected to; (c) tokenism, self-doubt, gender and race; and (d) resistance. This chapter will discuss these four themes.

Women of Color Ways of Knowing

An important theme in women of color mentorship is respecting our ways of knowing. Understanding and including women of color ways of knowing can decrease isolation and reject assimilation for both women of color students and women of color professionals in higher education. It is crucial to delve into the complexities and nuances of understanding and respecting the diverse ways of knowing within the women of color community. By recognizing and embracing these unique perspectives, we can create an environment that not only decreases feelings of isolation but also rejects assimilation as both students and professionals navigate academic spaces.

An important aspect of this theme is highlighted by Agosto et al. (2016), who emphasize the need for mentorship that supports women and demonstrates alternative ways of working and supporting one another within academia (p. 84). By breaking through the traditional "structure" of academic institutions, women of color can find empowerment and open new lines of thought, ultimately contributing to their personal and professional growth.

Agosto et al. (2016), states that breaking through the "structure" of academia involves engaging in mentorship that supports women and shows them there *are* different ways of showing up to class and work, as well as support one other in doing so, which can open new lines and modes of thought (p. 84). This idea of mentorship also supports women of color being able to avoid isolation that is so common and fosters an environment where women of color can continue to grow.

One powerful framework that aligns with women of color ways of knowing is Muxerista mentoring, extensively discussed by Alarcón and Bettez (2017) and Ek et al. (2010). Muxerista mentoring serves as a vehicle for leveraging the cultural wealth already possessed by Latinas, providing a space that validates the scholarship historically denied to women of color. Ek et al. (2010) describe Muxerista mentoring as a means to empower Latinas by embracing their unique ways of knowing (p. 31). Similarly, Alarcón and Bettez (2017) exemplify this framework by incorporating indigenous, feminist, and non-White ways of knowing in their research, thus highlighting the value and power of the scholarship Latinas bring to academia (p. 35).

Muxerista mentoring, discussed by both Alarcón and Bettez (2017) and Ek et al. (2010) is a powerful framework in supporting women of color ways of knowing. Ek et al. (2010) describe *Muxerista* mentoring as a "vehicle for leveraging the cultural wealth that Latinas already possess" (p. 31). This co-created mentorship space curates an environment of validation for women of color who have historically and continue to be denied their full engagement within the institution. Alarcón and Bettez (2017) are both women of color who work in a predominantly White institution (PWI), are similar in age, and both identify as multiracial Latina and White. In building on the framework of Ek et al. (2010) of *Muxerista* mentoring, Alarcón and Bettez actively practiced the framework and "'Browned' the space of research methodology by including material centering indigenous, feminist, and non-White ways of knowing and conducting research" (p. 35). This practice brings power and value to the work and scholarship that Latinas bring to the academy.

Respecting the ways of knowing specific to indigenous women is also a crucial aspect discussed in "Mentoring Women in Higher Education" by Paterson and Hart-Wasekeesikaw (1994). The authors emphasize the importance of mentoring that incorporates a feminist perspective of learning and knowing, challenging the traditional patriarchal structure of higher education. They argue that the knowledge held by indigenous women and women of color is incongruent with the traditional power dynamics within academia and should be empowered to embrace their multifaceted dimensions of knowing (p. 76).

Like understanding the Latina ways of knowing discussed above, Paterson and Hart-Wasekeesikaw (1994), discuss the importance of respecting indigenous women's ways of knowing in "Mentoring Women in Higher Education: Lessons from the Elders" (p. 76). Paterson and Hart-Wasekeesikaw (1994) state, "A call has been sounded for mentoring that incorporates the feminist perspective of learning and knowing" by moving away from reliance on the authority of professors as the sole holders of knowledge (p. 72). In this article, the authors also help us understand that the knowledge of indigenous women and other women of color are "incongruent with the traditional patriarchy of higher education" and should be empowered to embrace their many dimensions of knowing (p. 76).

To best describe how we can support women of color ways of knowing it is most important to create spaces of shared power and consider various types of knowing or epistemologies. When we are open to learning from our students and mentees, we share the power of knowledge through personal and cultural experiences and bring value to that knowledge. Cultivating this environment empowers learners who bring a diverse perspective to the academy, embrace their knowledge and see themselves as scholars within higher education. Women of color who are supported in this type of environment feel included, valued, and can bring that energy to their future learners as well.

To effectively support women of color ways of knowing, it is essential to create spaces of shared power. By recognizing the value of personal and cultural experiences, we can open ourselves to learning from our students and mentees, allowing for the exchange of diverse perspectives and knowledge. This inclusive environment empowers learners to embrace their unique ways of knowing, fostering a sense of inclusion and value within higher education. As a result, women of color who are supported in such environments feel empowered, valued, and are able to pass on that energy to future learners. We can gain insights and guidance to create supportive environments that honor and celebrate the diverse ways of knowing within the women of color community.

Finding a Community Women Feel Personally and Professionally Connected To

In this section of the literature review, we explore the theme of "finding a community women feel personally and professionally connected to" and its pivotal role in the success and retention of women of color (women of color) in higher education. The journey of women of color navigating academia can be filled with challenges and obstacles, making it essential to find a sense of belonging and hope within the academic environment, regardless of the role one plays.

Finding a sense of belonging and hope in academia as women of color in higher education, no matter the role that you play, is critical in their success and retention. McLane-Davison et al. (2017) shared the narratives of first-generation Black women scholars who built an accountability circle with other women who shared those same identities. This virtual community provided a safe and supportive circle of first-generation Black women scholars who supported each other and provided mentorship to each other through shared challenges and experiences in academia. This article is eye-opening in understanding allyship. Women of color are often told in one-on-one conversations with colleagues at their institutions that they are an ally, but when they are put in a public space where they can use their voice to support them, they remain silent. We see this through a clear example from Sistah 3 in the article, "I had allies among the faculty, although most of them were the silent type—those who supported me in my office but said nothing publicly when their voices could have helped me feel a sense of connectedness and value" (p. 26). This isn't a unique experience to one woman of color, but an experience that many women of color have in academia, which is why having this circle is transformational to their persistence and sense of hope in higher education.

McLane-Davison et al. (2017) shed light on the narratives of first-generation Black women scholars who created an accountability circle, forming a virtual community with other women who shared their identities. This safe and supportive circle became a vital source of mentorship and support, enabling them to navigate the shared challenges and experiences within academia. The article highlights the importance of allyship and the discrepancy between private affirmations of support and public silence. Sistah 3's experience illustrates how some colleagues who claimed to be allies remained silent when their voices could have made a significant impact in fostering a sense of connectedness and value (p. 26). This is not an isolated experience but a shared reality for many women of color in academia, making the formation of such circles transformational for their persistence and hope in higher education.

The experiences depicted in McLane-Davison et al. (2017) corroborate the findings of Nganga and Beck (2017), who explore the role of meaningful connectedness for women of color through three overarching themes: developing an academic and scholarly identity, battling a sense of place and belonging, and finding hope and regaining power and agency (pp. 557–563). All three themes encompass the perseverance women of color exhibit in academia despite facing self-doubt. The support and upliftment provided by fellow women of color not only foster their persistence in higher education but also instill hope as they confront daily challenges. Without a network of individuals who share similar identities and struggles, it becomes easy to succumb to hopelessness. However, gathering together to share frustrations, anger, and empower each other serves as a powerful reminder of what drives them to pursue higher education.

The experiences of women of color in McLane-Davison et al. (2017) proves much of what Nganga and Beck (2017) describe in the role of meaningful connectedness for women of color through three different themes: developing an academic and scholarly identity, battling a sense of place and belonging, and finding hope and regaining power and agency (pp. 557–563). All three of these themes describe persistence in academia through battling with self-doubt. Persistence, although hard to maintain, was supported by finding other women of color who supported and uplifted each other, which not only supported their persistence in academia, but brought them hope in dealing with daily challenges. It is easy to fall into hopelessness when there is not a network of individuals that share the same challenges and identities. Women of color can regain that sense of hope when they can gather to share their anger and frustrations yet empower each other to keep going by reminding each other of what keeps them in higher education.

Further insight into the empowering factors for women of color and what initially drew them to the field is found in Griffin's (2013) article, "Voices of the Othermothers: Reconsidering Black Professors' Relationships With Black Students as a Form of Social Exchange." Black professors, as highlighted by Griffin (2013), exhibit a deep passion for working with Black students and derive joy from witnessing their growth and development (p. 178). This reciprocal relationship not only allows Black professors to contribute to their students' development but also highlights the valuable insights and perspectives Black students bring to the research conducted by Black professors. Black students, equipped with a nuanced understanding of equity and access issues, provide invaluable contributions to the work and research within the Black professor's domain.

By exploring the literature surrounding the theme of finding a community women feel personally and professionally connected to, we gain deeper insights into the transformative power of support networks, allyship, and the significance of fostering a sense of belonging and hope within higher education. The subsequent sections of this literature review will delve into additional scholarly works, providing further perspectives and strategies to create inclusive and supportive environments that facilitate the personal and professional connections essential for the success and well-being of women of color in academia.

Some of the things that empower women of color and remind them what brought them into the field are shown in the article, "Voices of the Othermothers: Reconsidering Black Professors' Relationships With Black Students as a Form of Social Exchange" (Griffin, 2013). The common things for Black professors was the passion they had in working with Black students, and the joy it brought them in their development (p. 178). Griffin (2013) shows us the power of Black professors teaching Black students not only in allowing them to be a part of the development of their students, but in the contribution that Black students have to the research of Black professors. Black students understand equity and access issues more than their White peers, which brings valuable insight to the work and research of Black professors.

Tokenism, Self-Doubt, Gender, and Race

It is important to understand the battles that Black women and women of color face on a day to day, to truly understand how to support them.

Tokenism is one of the key contributors to women of color stressors in and out of the classroom. Women of color are often put in a position where they feel they need to prove themselves and as a result take on too many roles, which affects their physical and mental health. We see these examples in Chaney et al. (2011), Davis (2009), and Gregory (2001). In Chaney et al. (2011) they state, "When they overextend their time in these areas of service, they reduce their time to work on research and publication agendas" (p. 169). When they are soaked up by all of the additional responsibilities like serving on university committees and task forces, it takes away from their research time, which costs them their tenure (Chaney et al., 2011, p. 169). Again, Gregory (2001) provides us with the same insight on the number of responsibilities that Black women take on in higher education stating, "The barrier to Black faculty women's retention and advancement that is cited most often in the research is the extraordinary time demands placed upon them because of their relatively small numbers" (p. 134). Since there is most often a small number of Black women faculty, they are then tokenized and added to many additional groups and committees, which takes time away from their own professional development. Davis (2009) similarly states, "African American women are often treated as affirmative action tokens, compelling some to feel that they must prove themselves worthy. As a consequence, they take on too many tasks, often at the expense of their mental and physical health" (p. 55). We again see the same example of women of color taking on additional roles at a much higher cost and for positions that White professionals, especially men, do not have to work as hard for. Davis (2009) emphasizes the battles that women of color face because of both gender *and* race and the glass ceiling effect they face in education. They may attain higher positions in higher education, but they will still face unequal pay to men.

In this section of the literature review, we delve into the theme of "Tokenism, Self-Doubt, Gender, and Race (Intersectionality)" and its profound impact on the daily battles faced by Black women and women of color. To truly support and empower these individuals, it is crucial to comprehend the stressors they encounter on a day-to-day basis. Tokenism, specifically, emerges as a significant contributor to these stressors, affecting women of color both within and outside the classroom. Placed in positions where they constantly feel the need to prove themselves, women of color often find themselves shouldering excessive responsibilities that detrimentally impact their physical and mental well-being.

The presence of students of color, especially Black students, heavily depends on how women of color are treated and retained in higher education. I appreciated how Gregory (2001) in "Black Faculty Women in the

Academy: History, Status, and Future" underlines how supporting, or not supporting, Black women trickles down to the presence and experiences of students of color in higher education. Representation matters not just for the students and faculty that are already at the institution, but for prospective employees and students. To address these challenges, Gregory (2011) states, "We need to expand and support programs that provide real educational opportunities for students of all races, classes, and genders and demonstrate to these students, through example, the benefits of pursuing an academic career" (p. 135).

Insights from Chaney et al. (2011), Davis (2009), and Gregory (2001) illuminate the adverse consequences of tokenism on women of color. Chaney et al. (2011) highlight the challenge faced by women of color as they overextend themselves in various service areas, which, in turn, diminishes their time for research and publication agendas (p. 169). The additional responsibilities, such as serving on university committees and task forces, divert their focus from essential research endeavors, jeopardizing their prospects for tenure (Chaney et al., 2011, p. 169). Similarly, Gregory (2001) emphasizes the extraordinary time demands placed upon Black women faculty due to their relatively small numbers, becoming a barrier to their retention and advancement within higher education (p. 134). As tokenized individuals, Black women are often burdened with multiple roles and committee memberships, thereby impeding their own professional development.

Davis (2009) further underscores the experiences of African American women as they contend with being treated as affirmative action tokens, feeling compelled to prove their worthiness. Consequently, they undertake an excessive number of tasks, often at the expense of their mental and physical health (p. 55). This cycle perpetuates the inequality where women of color must exert significantly more effort than their White counterparts, particularly White men, to attain comparable positions. Davis (2009) accentuates the intersectionality of gender and race, shedding light on the glass ceiling effect that Black women face within the realm of education. Despite achieving higher positions in academia, they continue to encounter unequal pay in comparison to their male counterparts.

Moreover, the presence and experiences of students of color, particularly Black students, in higher education heavily depend on the treatment and retention of women of color. Gregory (2001) highlights the interconnection between supporting or neglecting Black women faculty and its implications for students of color within the academy. Representation plays a pivotal role not only for the current students and faculty at an institution but also for prospective employees and students. Addressing these challenges, Gregory (2011) emphasizes the need to expand and support programs that provide genuine educational opportunities for students of all races, classes, and genders. By doing so, these programs demonstrate to students the benefits of pursuing an academic career through tangible examples (p. 135).

By exploring the literature surrounding the theme of tokenism, self-doubt, gender, and race intersectionality, we gain a deeper understanding of the intricate struggles faced by Black women and women of color. These insights shed light on the detrimental impact of tokenism, the resulting burden of excessive responsibilities, and the overarching challenges rooted in gender and race inequalities. Recognizing the significance of representation and support in higher education is essential for fostering inclusive environments that uplift and empower women of color, thereby contributing to the success and well-being of both faculty and students of color. In the subsequent sections of this literature review, we will further examine scholarly works to gain additional perspectives and strategies to combat tokenism, dismantle self-doubt, and promote equity and inclusion within the higher education landscape.

Resistance

Persistence has been a common theme among women of color in higher education, which is further explained by *resistance*. In the article, "Resisting From the Margins: The Coping Strategies of Black Women and Other Women of Color Faculty Members at a Research University" Thomas and Hollenshead (2001) conducted a survey questioning how women of color managed to personally and professionally, cope with their marginalized position, and how they have used their position as a place of resistance to racism, sexism, and classism (p. 166). In their surveys they questioned women of color, White women, men of color, and White men. Their results confirmed that not only are the experiences of women of color far more challenging than their White counterparts, but also far more challenging than men of color (p. 172). These challenges were explained by five different themes that women of color focus groups brought together: organizational barriers, institutional climate, lack of respect from one's colleagues, unwritten rules that govern university life, and mentoring (pp. 168–175). Some of the organizational barriers that women of color experience are manipulation by their institution. They are used for the institution's agenda, and do not offer positions (and pay) for what they are truly worth. This treatment by the institutions then fosters an unhealthy institutional climate for women of color. Pamela, one of the respondents of the survey shared that the university "does not like outsiders" (p. 170). She explains that because the university does not like outsiders, she is then always the person confronting people who says something that she doesn't agree with, which then becomes an extremely exhausting role (p. 170). Women of color internalize their oppression and either leave or remain in their positions always wondering what they did wrong. There needs to be opportunities for women of color to step back and look objectively at their own work and the work of other women of color who fall under that same trap. This space is also critical because of Thomas and Hollenshead's (2001) third theme: lack of respect from one's colleagues. Respondents in this survey frequently reported that they were asked to change their interests and agendas to "fit in" with others in their units. This was a key place where resistance was critical. Resisting this pressure is what makes a difference in the research that is culturally relevant to people of color. The fourth theme, which shines light in one of the many issues of White elitist academia, which are the unwritten rules that women of color are expected to adhere to but not informed about. One of the examples from a respondent was the pressure to write only for academic audiences, when she strived to have accessible writing that *any* person outside of academia. The other example described frequently when examining women of color in higher education is protection of service time (p. 173). Women of color are too often unable to protect their time because they have many additional responsibilities, advising, serving on committees, and more. Women of color being on campus in small numbers, feel the pressures to be more involved to make sure that the voices of the communities that belong to are heard. White professionals can protect their time because they do not have the pressure to represent their groups. The last theme in this article is mentoring. Thomas and Hollenshead (2001), Clayborne and Hamrick (2007), and Nganga and Beck (2017) describe mentorship as a resistance group. Having a mentor or a mentorship group of women of color who share the same or similar experiences at their institutions is a powerful way for women to channel their anger and frustrations to resist the pressures they carry and help ground each other in their work. A comment from a respondent, "You need to find the community of color in [your local area] so that you can look at some people and see yourself reflected, because in your professional life at [a predominantly White] university, you will not see that" (Thomas & Hollenshead, 2001, p. 175). In the end, women of color must sustain their confidence in their skills no matter what goes on around them. They must actively choose to resist and choose to persist in their work. Mentorship groups help women of color get there.

    The theme of resistance emerges as a significant aspect of understanding the experiences of women of color (women of color) in higher education. Persistence, a common theme among women of color, is further elucidated through the lens of resistance. In the article titled "Resisting From the Margins: The Coping Strategies of Black Women and Other Women of Color Faculty Members at a Research University," Thomas and Hollenshead (2001) conducted a survey to explore how women of color navigate their marginalized positions, cope personally and professionally, and utilize their position as a site of resistance against racism, sexism, and classism (p. 166). The survey included participants from various groups, including women of color, White women, men of color, and White men. The results confirmed that the experiences of women of color not only surpassed the challenges faced by their White counterparts but were also more demanding than those encountered by men of color (p. 172).

The survey data generated five key themes identified by women of color focus groups: organizational barriers, institutional climate, lack of respect from colleagues, unwritten rules governing university life, and mentoring (pp. 168–175). Organizational barriers encompass manipulative practices by institutions, exploiting women of color for their own agendas while undervaluing their worth. Consequently, an unhealthy institutional climate is fostered, as revealed by Pamela, one of the survey respondents, who stated that the university "does not like outsiders" (p. 170). This leads women of color to assume the exhausting role of confronting people who express views with which they disagree (p. 170). women of color often internalize their oppression, causing them to question their abilities and contemplate leaving their positions. To counter this, opportunities must be created for women of color to objectively assess their work and that of other women of color caught in the same trap.

The lack of respect from colleagues, the third theme, becomes a critical site for resistance. Survey respondents frequently reported being pressured to align their interests and agendas with those of others in their units, compromising their unique perspectives. Resisting this pressure is vital for producing research that is culturally relevant to people of color. The fourth theme sheds light on one of the many issues within White elitist academia: the unwritten rules that women of color are expected to adhere to but are not explicitly informed about. For instance, women of color may face pressure to write exclusively for academic audiences, whereas they strive for accessible writing that reaches beyond the confines of academia. Additionally, women of color often struggle to protect their time due to numerous additional responsibilities, such as advising and committee work. Unlike their White counterparts, who do not face the same pressure to represent their groups, women of color find it challenging to safeguard their time (p. 173).

Mentoring, the last theme explored in this article, is portrayed as a form of resistance. Thomas and Hollenshead (2001), along with Clayborne and Hamrick (2007) and Nganga and Beck (2017), highlight the transformative power of mentorship as a resistance group. Establishing mentorship connections or groups with women of color who share similar experiences within their institutions provides a powerful outlet for channeling anger and frustration, grounding each other in their work. A respondent emphasizes the importance of finding a community of color in their local area to see oneself reflected, as the predominantly White university environment often fails to provide such representation (Thomas & Hollenshead, 2001, p. 175). Ultimately, women of color must sustain their confidence in their skills amidst challenging circumstances, actively choosing to resist and persist in their work. Mentorship groups play a vital role in supporting women of color on this journey.

By exploring the theme of resistance, we gain valuable insights into the coping strategies and acts of defiance employed by women of color in higher education. These insights shed light on the organizational barriers, institutional climate, lack of respect, unwritten rules, and mentoring that shape the experiences of women of color. Understanding the complexities and challenges faced by women of color provides a foundation for implementing supportive measures and fostering an inclusive academic environment.

We consider mentorship as a learning experience leading us to engage with teaching pedagogy. Liberatory relationships can take the form of mentorship through intentional use of critical teaching pedagogy; supporting development of self-authorship mentorship that acknowledge power, situates the individual in the system to learn and develop through so that persistence in higher education can be achieved with the least amount of marginalization (Baxter Magolda & King, 2004; hooks, 1998; Rendón, 2008; Snipes & LePeau, 2017). Through approaching mentorship with critical pedagogies, these relationships have developed into spaces of transformative learning, liberation, and as sites as resistance to the systemic power and inequities at a predominantly White institution.

While there is much research about mentorship, the term is unsettling for each of the researchers and does not adequately describe our relationship. This research study sought to gain insight into the uniqueness of our relationships, to identify characteristics, and name the multigenerational mentorship experiences that we have together. Our experiences as women of color attending, working at, and resisting from the margins of a predominantly White institution as well as our pedagogical notions of education have deeply connected us and shaped our experiences (Squire et al., 2016).

From this original research study, the core themes and valuable attributes necessary for the success of these relationships expanded into a newly developed model. The theoretical model of women of color transformational mentorship is presented in detail to describe such relationships and inspire others to intentionally facilitate similar partnerships.

Critical Pedagogy

An important component of college is self-authorship, which is the ability for one to explore and decide on their beliefs in a way that their identity and engagement are aligned (Baxter Magolda & King, 2004). These mutual relations can come through liberatory notions of education, learning partnerships, and education spaces in which students can be co-constructors of knowledge (Friere, 1970; hooks, 1998; Rendón, 2008; Snipes & LePeau, 2017). Teaching pedagogies have been developed that center the student, positions the educator as a co-learner, and that hold community and reflection as key components (hooks, 1994; Rendón, 2008). Sentipensante pedagogy (Rendon, 2008) and engaged pedagogy (hooks, 1994) center educators and students of color, first generation, and other communities historically denied access to higher ed. As we re-image work with students, we as educators can use tools of liberation to rupture the status quo and create transformative experiences for students.

Much of our work with students, which we approach in a way that engages the whole student, is liberatory, and at its core, is justice work. Such scholars, Friere (1970), hooks (1998), and Rendón (2008) discuss liberatory pedagogies in the context of the classroom, but not other teaching forms. Rendón (2008) provides *sentipensante* pedagogy integrating sensing and thinking into our learning connecting to ways people have been learning for centuries. This liberatory learning approach is a union of sensing and thinking and engages intuition, subjectiveness, contemplation, human community, humanism, and personal development (Rendón, 2008). hooks (1998) provides through engaged pedagogy that educating so any person can learn is "the practice of freedom" (p. 13) and is essential for our most deep learning. We, as educators, are called to be healers and teach students how to "live in the world" (p. 15). Engaged pedagogy asks educators to be vulnerable, share, and to "make their teaching practices a site of resistance" (hooks, 1998, p. 21).

Both Rendón (2008) and hooks' (1998) work centers both individuals and the learning community and ask us as educators to provide and create spaces that are liberatory and transformative through engaging with students as whole beings who bring knowledge that the entire learning community, including faculty, can learn from. Knowing this, our research provides a way to approach mentorship relationships as teaching spaces where both individuals are able to bring their full selves, experience deep learning, and liberate their work in higher education.

In conclusion, this chapter has provided an introductory exploration of the literature on mentorship within communities of color in higher education. By delving into the existing research, we have gained valuable insights into the individuals who have been the focus of study, the various types of mentorship that have been examined, and the broader scholarly context in which our own work is situated. Through this exploration, we have highlighted the importance of critically examining mentorship practices and adopting a pedagogical approach that empowers individuals from marginalized communities. Our critical pedagogical lens has led us to embrace the concept of liberationships, which go beyond traditional mentorship models and facilitate transformative growth, identity shifts, and purposeful contributions beyond the confines of higher education. By recognizing the cyclical nature of growth, fostering self-awareness, and embracing personal leadership, women of color can navigate their journeys with intention and resilience. Through liberationships, they can develop the confidence, skills, and agency necessary to create meaningful change and contribute to a more inclusive and equitable society. By expanding the conversation on mentorship and elevating the voices and experiences of communities of color, we can collectively work towards a future where mentorship is empowering, transformative, and liberatory for all.

5

Why Mentorship?

In this chapter, we delve into the rich historical context of marginalized communities within higher education and explore the profound significance of transformative and liberatory relationships. By examining the ways in which marginalized individuals have built relationships in their communities for support, sustenance, and resistance, we aim to shed light on the essential role of liberationships in education. Through an exploration of historical narratives and personal accounts, we advocate for the necessity of nurturing transformative relationships that empower marginalized individuals and foster a more inclusive and equitable academic environment.

Historical Context of Minoritized Communities Within Higher Education

In the spirit of Black women, who for generations, have been using stories to "instruct, direct, protect, and survive," we offer two poems written by Kim as part of her literature review for her dissertation work examining virtual women of color mentorship (Edwards, 2018, p. 86). Songs, poems, and testimonios have been used by Black and Latina scholars to "bring light to brutality, build solidarity, and narrate the liberation of their communities" (McAloney, 2021, p. 20). In the spirit of these foremothers, we share these poems. The first is a historical piece discussing higher education's beginning as well as a summation of mentorship literature. The second and third poems will be shared later in this chapter.

> **Foundations**
>
> What higher ed was built on?
>
> Religion. Politics.
> Assimilation. Genocide.
> Slavery. Exclusion.
>
> To educate elite white Christian men
> To drive colonies, townships, churches
> To set their standards of specific types of leaders
> Leaders who would fight for life
> (of some)
> Leaders who would fight for liberty
> (of some)
> Leaders who would fight for the pursuit of happiness
> (of some)
> And leaders who would encourage Manifest Destiny
>
> To assimilate Tribal communities
> The stripping of hair, practices, language, culture
> To force Native peoples to live
> Civili-no, white.
> But then
> It wasn't adequate
> Claiming they weren't enough
> Claiming there was something just not quite right
> Using education to justify...
> Death.
>
> It was a criminal act to teach
> Black people

Punishable by death
Their bodies built
Literally laid the physical foundations
But then
It wasn't adequate
Claiming they weren't enough
Claiming there was something just not quite right
Using research to justify...
Hatred.

How *did* higher education come about?

Religion. Politics.
Assimilation. Genocide.
Slavery. Exclusion.

These upper class values
Middle class values that are
Pervasive
Throughout
Higher
Education
Built on this foundation
This Christian-ness
This whiteness
informs our structure
Our curriculum
Our research
Our teaching

As we raise the next generation of educators
We teach
We advise
We counsel
We intern
We apprentice
We mentor

Two ways mentorship is talked about:
Banking and Easing

I'm the knower
I've been there
Banking is me teaching you
Banking is me sharing my experiences with you
You sit and listen
You sit and observe
You sit and ask questions
You sit and learn

Banking be white
whiteness demands:
Be like me
Fit the mold

Easing comes across differently
Differently shows up with intentionality
Around
marginalized communities
Communities where a mentor has been there and
There, a mentor can ease you into what it's going to be like

From Black women easing Black women into faculty roles with discretion
From Harper easing Black men through the doctoral progression
From NUFP mentors easing folx into the student affairs profession
They've been there
They've done it
They live it

Easing mentors have insight, their thoughts
Their stories, experiences
Around
Navigating, managing, combating
Heterosexism
Ableism
Whiteness

Easing
Easing because they are easing others into the field
Easing into how to navigate upper- and middle-class values
Easing into how to navigate the Christian-ness
Easing into how to navigate the whiteness

Can mentorship look transformational?
Can it look different?
Can a mentor learn from a mentee?
I'm not just talkin about light learnin but
LEARNING
Can it be more?
Can a mentee impact the out-of-work decisions of a mentor?
How do we change our thinking?
New realities
Create new spaces
Spaces of liberation and what they look like

In the past 400 years
We've come a-ways
Higher education is more...
Looks more diverse
Higher education is changing
We are changing
(Reprinted with permission, McAloney, 2021)

To truly understand the importance of transformative and liberatory relationships, we must first examine the historical struggles faced by minoritized communities in higher education. Originally, higher education in the United States was built and designed for theology and the assimilation of Indigenous communities to dominant U.S. culture. As Indigenous students graduated from the early academic institutions, the White ruling class decided that while Indigenous students in dress, in language, in action, and in education were similar to the White graduates, the Indigenous graduates were still not White. This was the turning point for higher education and its relationship with Indigenous communities; instead of a relationship of assimilation, it became one of exclusion.

Exclusion was not unfamiliar to communities of color during this colonial period of U.S. higher education. The White supremacist and racial capitalist foundation of the United States is the same foundation of colleges and universities. As such, the Black community was also excluded as students from higher education. This specificity of the Black community not being able to be "students" is important here as, because of this White supremacist and racial capitalist foundation along with the U.S. invention of chattel enslavement, Black folks built these institutions of higher ed in two ways. The first way the Black community unwillingly supported the development of these early institutions was through enslaved labor that literally built brick and mortar buildings on those early campuses. The second way the Black community unwillingly supported the development of these early institutions is through the sale of enslaved individuals to fund them. Finally, it is important to note that the enslaved worked to care for people (faculty, staff, and students), the institution (grounds, preparing and serving food, cleaning, etc.), and the land of these early colonial institutions. Colonial institutions survived and thrive today because of these, largely unrecognized, contributions and unrecognized labor and sacrifice. These universities and colleges founded back during this early time, most of which we now call the "Ivy League" held so much exclusion that continues today.

This notion of Whiteness, along with its sibling mentioned earlier, patriarchy, came to be an important component to who would be allowed to enter into these academic institutions. This distinction allowed for certain groups to be kept outside of higher education. Both those who were kept out as well as the gatekeepers understood the power of the academic space—students experiencing critical thinking, engaging in college-level work at the institution. This denial of educational access allowed the wealthy, White male ruling class to continue to deny educational access. This denial of educational access supported the current system with the distinctions of the ruling class and the working class or workers as well as women. This allowed the ruling class to continue to govern and rule over women and the working class. This was the continuation of colonization; which for the United States meant genocide of Indigenous Peoples and the enslavement of Black communities. This access, or lack thereof, is still present today. Let's talk a bit more about how we got to where we are now.

History of Women in Higher Education

The United States was slow in educating women collegiately as women were believed to have intellectual inferiority than men and that college would press cultural buttons for women who were destined to be wives and mothers (Peril, 2006; Renn, 2014). It wasn't until 1837 until women were permitted to enroll in any college. Oberlin admitted women in order to "provide ministers with intelligent, cultivated, and thoroughly schooled wives" (Peril, 2006, p. 30). Over time, the Catholic church shifted their concern around admitting women to college to holding that educating women could then become educated women that could instruct their children. A quote that sums this time up well: "Any girl who lets herself forget the fact that one important use of an education is to help her toward achieving a happy marriage, a home, and a family—the things she really wants—is being a very foolish virgin indeed" (Peril, 2006, p. 10). This cultural shift led to not only considering that women could use their education to instruct their children, but to also find a husband to father those children.. Here, women were encouraged to go to college to find husbands and were educated largely on how to be a good hostess and as to not appear smarter than her husband (Graham, 1978; Miller-Bernal & Paulson, 2007).

Women had been seen as controllable, vulnerable creatures that would be affected by any type of mishap, and that any mishap or addition to their role within the home would influence their reproductive system. During this time, there was also a widespread belief that women attending college harmed their reproductive organs (Miller-Bernal & Paulson, 2007). Samuel Mitchell, a professor and medical doctor, said that a woman experiencing shocks during conception or irritation of the mind can influence the appearance of her child (Wilder, 2013). He went on to say that after a woman found out their favorite domestic animal died, she would later give birth to a "deformed" infant (Wilder, 2013). Today, women are still presented as a sort of property of the family or man. Of course, this is in connection to cultural, social and religious beliefs that continue to limit the accessibility of women.

With the Civil War needing more soldiers, colleges and universities needed tuition-paying undergraduate women in order to survive. This led to a rise in the enrollment of women students to 21% (Graham, 1978). In 1905, Theodore Roosevelt posited that educated women would be less likely to have children and get married which would cause a "race suicide." Similarly, there was still negative thinking around women attending college particularly co-educationally. This negative idea around co-education was that the co-educational space would cause damage through either contributing to indifference of women to male-identified students because of overfamiliarity and/or that co-educational species would encourage promiscuity (Miller-Bernal & Paulson, 2007).

It wasn't just the intelligence of women that really scared men (college administrators, governmental leaders, etc.). The blue stocking woman who wanted to go to school to college challenged the image of femininity that was idealized in that day. This image of femininity included a woman submissive to her husband, taking care of her family, and being totally happy in her home and the duties around her home (Perril, 2006).

Black Women's Experiences

Until this point in this chapter, we've discussed women broadly. During these times, women referred specifically to White women. Let's shift focus to women of color. The most robust amount of literature is around Black women struggling to be admitted into and then survive and thrive in college. During the time co-education was controversial in White communities, historically Black colleges and universities (HBCUs) admitted men and women students from their beginning (Peril, 2006). Co-educaton was more economical and provided more resources for the institution and while White women were bound by the "ideas of true womanhood that made homebound domesticity a woman's highest achievement," Black women were often excluded from preparatory courses that were part of entrance eligibility requirements for college and were kept out of schools that were more prestigious and offered graduate school preparation (Evans, 2007). Colleges and universities that did admit Black women, often had quotas. Civil rights activist Dorthy Height was denied entrance to Barnard in 1933 after arriving for the admissions interview and the institution finding out at that moment that she was Black. Her application was denied because Barnard had already admitted two Black students meeting their quota for that year (Evans, 2016).

Because of racial capitalism and White supremacy, Black women's experiences in the collegiate classroom, once they overcame the barrier of admissions, Black women reported feeling "fear, insecurity, and pressure in an atmosphere that not only was competitive, but where White students and instructors doubted their intellectual capability" (Evans, 2016. p. 52). Though Black collegiate women praises were sung, there were constant blocks around their self-determination and independence. Black women were pressured to "be scholarly (but not too smart), fashionable (but not gaudy), and any number of other contradictions" (Evans, 2016, p. 57) was ever-present. These contradictions are still incredibly present for women of color students, professionals working on campuses, and professionals today.

Essential Role of Transformative and Liberatory Relationships

My Journey Into Higher Education

When I joined NUFP as an undergrad
I thought we were cared about
I thought we were priority

I thought higher ed was about change
Making the world a better place
But as I began my Master's program
Your true face came through
Reality set in
And I began to ask myself:
Do *Black* women's lives matter in higher education?
Do Black *women's* lives matter in higher education?

Do I matter in your classroom?
Do you want to hear my voice?
Not speaking on behalf of all people, but
Me
I speak for me
My truth
My narrative
My experience
My story
Is that what you're interested in?
No
No, it's not

Oh, what do Black folks think about this, you ask
But you don't call on my hand
Instead you just ignore me or
Is it that you don't see me
Oh, that's right
It's not what you're interested in
Imma sit right here and once again be silent in your classroom
Oh, what's the Black perspective you ask?
Mmmmm
Imma sit here and once again be silent in your classroom

Do Black women's lives matter in higher education?
Yes, I'm faculty
Yes, I'm qualified
Yes, I'm educated

I forget for a second
You don't really mean Black women's lives matter
You don't really mean Black women's lives matter
YOU DON'T REALLY MEAN BLACK WOMEN'S LIVES MATTER

You don't respect me
You don't trust me
You don't hold my truth
Listen to my story

You don't value me. My colleagues.
My students. My people.
My ancestors.
Students and faculty
Who came before us
Who you also dismissed
Told this place was not for us

Just as Mary Church Terrell experienced
Blood is thicker than water
And we still traverse through education
As the sacred Black cow in the footsteps of
Zora Neale Hurston
Documented through I, too, Am Harvard
Our struggle continues
"Having an opinion does not make me an 'Angry Black Woman'"
"I am not 'pulling the race card'. You're just being racist."
"'I don't see color' Does that mean you don't see me?"
Do you see me as "incognegro"?
Do Black women's lives matter in higher education?

Do Black women's lives matter in higher education?
No
No, I think not but we could
Be free from the debt that will chain us
Free to share of our single and collective stories
Free to speak in the classroom

See ourselves represented by who and what is in front of us
To not be asked who we are
To not be asked what our experience is
To not be interrogated for our every move
To sit at the table
To have
Dare I say it
A reimagined shared power
Yup, I said it: shared power
A shared vision of what
Of who we could be
We, Black folk
We <u>all</u> of us at the university
Do Black women's lives matter in higher education?
(McAloney, 2021, reprinted with permission)

As discussed in the last chapter, there is a gap in literature in mentoring professionals and students of color in higher education and mentorship of women of color. This gap in the literature provides an opportunity for a new approach that brings together "mentorship, critical pedagogy, liberation, and process" (McAloney, 2021). Through the liberatory mentorship for women of color model (McAloney & Long, 2019), we hope to provide a more expansive understanding of the types of liberatory relationships that can exist in higher education not only for survival, but for thrivance (Jollivette, 2020). This work offers deep insight into the power of critical mentorship, critical relationships, and the transformation that can come because of them. Our work provides a counternarrative for forming and participating in mentorship experiences. This supportive relationship can push the bounds of traditional mentorship that are limiting and provide a structure for growth of all engaged within the relationship.

This combination of mentorship, critical pedagogy, liberation, and process push us to constant growth and change. This growth and change is not only internal, but is also external. The internal work allows us to find community and validation within the relationship that help correct the hold of hegemony and internalized oppressions. Because of this internal work, we are able to find strength and support to change and grow externally. The external work includes supporting one another for engaging differently in the classroom or workspace. This includes the opportunity to try out different approaches, responses, and creativity. This external engagement then allows us to be more aligned with ourselves, our pedagogy, and our vision for ourselves and the work we do which lead to an increase of work productivity or contributions. These contributions could include deeper relationships, publishing and writing, new positions and promotions, and so much more.

Our experiences as multiracial women of color from low-income classes of origin along with our engagement in this growth work, position us to find a place to belong despite the constant othering of the institution. From this place of belonging, we can choose and are equipped to deny or resist systemic oppression. This curated place of belonging and dialogue allow for a self-affirmation of who we are individually and as socially constructed group members that shape why we are the way that we are. We are able to engage and consider our stories as gifts and wisdom. We, then, get to share these gifts with one another to learn from each other, to continue to hone the wisdom from our stories. It's through this reciprocity of sharing and reflecting which allow us to engage in co-learning in the co-created space together. This space then becomes a healing space. As we continue to work toward our individual and collective healing and liberation, this place of belonging and liberationship become a space to dream and vision.

Liberationships are built on a foundation of connection with shared identities and collaboration opportunities through helping one another become aware of and support through new opportunities. As such, we are explicitly to share about our identities with the ability not only to name our identities, but to also explore the systems of power and oppression that are at play in the institutional environment. This is reinforced through continual validation leading to our individual and collective growth allowing us to increase our contributions to ourselves, one another, and everything we engage in professionally and personally.

This learning from one another and teaching one another that happens through reflection opens up an accepting and supportive space. This is the critical pedagogy component that the mentor or teacher can facilitate a learning environment that is both student–teacher and teacher–student (Freire, 1970). Our desire for growth and connection to one another allow for us to invest time into the liberationships. This time investment is a commitment to wanting to grow individually and collectively together. This facilitated learning environment carries a shared desire for equity, inclusion, and belonging and a value of self-reflection and personal growth. Engaging in this self-reflection and personal growth in a community of like-minded women helps us see things differently, to grow, and to expand our perspectives because of the trust, authenticity, and investment we have made within our relationships. This is transformational mentorship. This is liberationship.

As we wrap up this first section of the book, we wanted to share that writing this book is a love letter to our previous selves. It carries what has happened in our experiences, what might happen in yours, and tips for success. We offer a reflexive and reciprocal praxis pushing us to engage as scholar practitioners. We have transformed through these liberationships. Our mindset and goals have transformed. Our work has transformed. Our identities have transformed. We have faced and are overcoming the imposter syndrome through our process of naming and acknowledging power dynamics that then have allowed us to deepen our view of ourselves as we currently are and as we evolve and transform. We began to get stronger in resisting the stories we heard and were told about ourselves. We were able to find purpose and a niche to make our space a space we can bring more of our whole selves. We share story authentically. We engage with resistance to systems of power together. We can't wait to continue sharing with you!

Transformational Women of Color Relationships

Connection.
Relationship.
Intentionality.
Authenticity.
Honesty.

I feel heard.
Learning from and with you.

In our work together, I grow
In our work together, I reflect
In our work together, I center

In our conversations, I feel more understood
In our conversations, I feel more grounded
In our conversations, I feel more affinity

Because of you, I think differently
Because of you, I think deeply
Because of you, I act intentionally

These organic relationships
Shaped me
My personal self
My professional self

How do we name?
How do we name this relationship?
How do we name this experience?

Connection
Relationship
Intentionality

At first, awkward
But then it flowed
The depth of our conversation
A conversation that feeds my soul

How do we name the whiteness and masculinity
Associated with the term mentorship

How do we name?
How do we name *this*?
How do we name *this* experience?

This is why we do this work

Authenticity
Honesty

These organic relationships
Shaped me

All of me

My person self
My professional self
My spiritual self
My woman of color self
My first generation self
We have depth.
We have connection.
We have created a new space
A space of liberation
Of transformation

Connection.
Relationship.
Intentionality.
Authenticity.
Honesty.
(McAloney, 2021, reprinted with permission)

# 6

"Considerations and Recommendations"

In this chapter we will present two sections detailing how to implement the model; one section will be written with considerations and recommendations for mentors, and the second for mentees. We will highlight how each consideration and recommendation aligns with the different layers of the model to demonstrate its importance, provide language, and prepare for deeper application of the model. As we consider liberationships a learning space, we can pull from bell hooks and Laura Rendón's theories of engaging in the classroom in critical ways. With this, the mentor is the facilitator of the space opening it up to co-create the formats of the time together and the topics to discuss. This happens through reflection, reciprocity, and resistance. Given such, we provide our recommendations within those three areas.

Section 1: Considerations and Recommendations for Mentors

Reflection

One of the primary ways of communicating via a liberationship is through reflection. For us, reflection incorporates establishing trust and building rapport, building safety and trust that the other person is taking care of their own needs (by modeling this, discussing this, empowering each other to do so), co-creating use of your time together and topics to discuss based on previous experiences that are pertinent, nurturing self-reflection and critical thinking, and goal setting together to identify areas you need support, training, lessons, and guidance. Throughout this section, we'll engage with these ideas.

As a mentor, it is essential to establish trust and build rapport through creating a safe and open space for your mentee to reflect on their experiences with you. Begin by sharing of and about yourself and your own journey. This will model the way you hope your mentee will communicate openly with you. As the mentor, you have a position of power and authority in this role, as mentorship traditionally values your role over that of the mentee, and your mentee may be entering your liberationship with that view in mind. Given this, your willingness to share vulnerably sets the tone for how deep your relationship can go. As your mentee begins sharing, practice actively listening and showing genuine interest in their experiences, goals, and challenges. Ask follow up questions to deeper understand their experience and support them to reflect further about their lessons learned. Asking follow up questions opens lines of communication, and demonstrates empathy and respect. To fully be present and show empathy and respect, you will need to also monitor and take care of your own needs. Furthermore, you should be encouraging your mentee to do the same. Model this, discuss what it means to care for oneself, and empower each other to do it through mutual reflections. By fostering a supportive and inclusive communication environment, you lay the foundation for a transformative mentorship journey.

Listen attentively to your mentees, providing them with undivided attention and demonstrating genuine interest in their experiences, goals, and challenges. Engage with them about their journey, goals, and experiences. Active listening helps create a safe and supportive space for mentees to share their thoughts and concerns. As you actively listen, empathize with your mentees' experiences, acknowledging the unique challenges they may face as individuals from marginalized communities. Share from your own experiences that align through similarity or that you are able to empathize from, but be mindful not to downplay their feelings or experiences, again, monitoring your position of power during the early period of your relationship's development. Demonstrating this understanding and empathy helps foster trust and rapport within the mentorship relationship. As you engage with mentees, engage in the relationship with a non-judgmental attitude and respect for their mentees. Appreciate the diversity of perspectives and backgrounds your mentees bring, treating them with dignity, and valuing their lived experiences. It is from these experiences that you will be able to reciprocally grow and learn from your mentee.

Though we think this is a given, we do want to specifically name that you should maintain the confidentiality of the information shared during your conversations, creating a trustworthy environment where everyone feels comfortable sharing their thoughts, concerns, and aspirations without fear of judgment or disclosure. Keep the details within your relationship and take away from the conversations lessons learned that you can then share. If needed, contact any program coordinators for support you may need navigating difficult conversational topics or to find resources that may be available to further support your mentee.

As it is important for there to be a shared identity with the mentees, there can also be incredible diversity within the liberationship as well. Familiarize yourself with the cultural backgrounds, identities, and experiences of your mentees, being mindful of potential biases or assumptions. Promote an inclusive approach that values and respects the diversity of mentees. Google questions and/or find another person with shared identities as your mentee to engage in learning with. It is not your mentee's role to teach you about their culture or identities. There is a level of engaging in thoughtful conversation with your mentees about their identities and cultures, space to ask questions, and for you to share as well. This space should be a mutually sharing space and allow for nuances. An example might be Googleing when Persian New Year is, but then having a conversation with your mentee about if their family engages with it, and if they do then follow up to ask about how they and/or their family, specifically, celebrates the holiday. The ability to bring one's whole self to the liberationship is validating and allows for growth. Open the space up to share identities and cultures with a thoughtful lens.

hooks (1998) calls us to continue the path as educators to our own self-actualization. This happens largely through our own continued learning and development. This growth is not only an example for your mentee, but a key component of liberationships. Stay informed about issues relevant to your mentees' experiences, engage in justice, equity, diversity, inclusion, access, and belonging training, and seek opportunities to enhance your critical mentoring (and teaching) skills.

Establish regular check-ins with your mentees and engage in goal setting. Regular communication and check-ins help to maintain the momentum of the relationship, while goal setting allows both of you to define and work towards their aspirations with the guidance of one another. Sometimes this goal setting can be loose and others can be very specific. By incorporating these elements into their mentorship approach, mentors can contribute to the transformative and empowering experiences of their mentees.

In conclusion of the reflection section, we recommend that you seek to facilitate opportunities for your mentee to engage in self-reflection and critical thinking to promote spaces for you two to develop deeper connections. Encourage your mentee to question assumptions, explore alternative viewpoints, and develop a deeper understanding of themselves and the world around them. Foster a growth mindset that promotes intellectual curiosity and a commitment to lifelong learning by asking questions they may not have considered yet.

Reciprocity

To engage in reciprocity, mentors can demonstrate providing constructive feedback, sharing of resources and opportunities, and providing guidance in navigating the challenges. As you demonstrate these skills, ask your mentee for support through these channels as well in support of your own goals. Ask them to let you know of resources or opportunities connected to learning in alignment with your professional and/or personal goals. Ask your mentee to provide you with their perspective, opinion and/or feedback on your current work projects. Typically, mentorship relationships have some sort of power dynamics within them, especially at the beginning, even when seeking to approach the mentorship through the lens of a liberationship. As such, it's important to provide specific opportunities for mentees to share their opinions, make their own decisions, all while offering support and guidance along the way so that they feel empowered and welcome also do the same for you. Use feedback as an opportunity to reflect on your progress and make necessary adjustments.

Recognize the diversity and intersectionality of your mentee's identity and experiences. Approach your mentorship relationship by embracing cultural humility, acknowledging your own biases and committing to ongoing learning. Foster an inclusive and equitable mentorship relationship that values and celebrates differences. By embracing diversity, you contribute to the transformative potential of the mentorship model. Furthermore, you should consider how your and your mentees' identities intersect and influence your experiences.

Recognizing and honoring the diversity and intersectionality of your mentee's identity and experiences is crucial for creating an inclusive and equitable mentorship relationship. As a mentor, it is essential to approach the mentorship journey with cultural humility, acknowledging that you have your own biases and committing to ongoing learning. Embracing this mindset allows you to cultivate a safe space where your mentee feels seen, heard, and valued.

To foster an inclusive mentorship relationship that engages in reciprocity, it is important to value and share your differences. Each participant of a liberationships relationship brings a unique set of backgrounds, perspectives, and lived experiences that enrich the learning process. By embracing diversity, you contribute to the transformative potential of the mentorship model. Emphasize the importance of creating an environment that appreciates and respects differences, ensuring that your mentee's voice and contributions are recognized and uplifted.

In addition to recognizing diversity, it is crucial to consider the intersections of your own and your mentees' identities. Our identities are multifaceted, influenced by various social, cultural, and personal factors. Acknowledging these intersections allows for a deeper understanding of the complex challenges and opportunities your mentee may encounter. By actively engaging with these intersections, you can offer more nuanced guidance and support that addresses the unique needs and experiences of your mentee, as well as opening space for you to share about your own experiences that show how you have navigated similar situations.

As you embark on the mentorship journey, be open to learning from your mentee. Recognize that knowledge and wisdom can flow in both directions, and that your mentee's experiences and perspectives are valuable sources of insight. Encourage your mentee to share their opinions, ideas, and feedback on your current work projects. Creating a reciprocal space where both mentor and mentee can learn from each other not only empowers your mentee, but also allows you to grow and develop in your own professional and personal goals.

In order to foster an inclusive and equitable mentorship relationship, it is important to establish clear communication channels that invite your mentee's input and decision-making. Actively involve your mentee in setting goals, designing strategies, and making decisions related to their academic and professional journey. By providing space for your mentee to exercise autonomy and agency, you empower them to take ownership of their own growth and development.

Furthermore, be mindful of the power dynamics inherent in mentorship relationships, especially at the beginning. While seeking to approach the mentorship through the lens of a liberationship, acknowledge that the mentor may hold a position of power and privilege. Actively mitigate these dynamics by creating opportunities for your mentee to exercise their own agency, make their own decisions, and express their opinions. Strive to create a mentorship relationship that is grounded in collaboration, respect, and mutual growth.

Remember, mentorship is not a one-size-fits-all approach. Each mentee is unique, and their needs may vary. Flexibility and adaptability are key in providing personalized support. Continuously reflect on your mentorship practices, seeking feedback from your mentee and utilizing self-reflection to improve your approach.

Emphasizing the importance of understanding and appreciating the complexity of your mentee's identity is crucial for creating a truly inclusive and supportive mentorship relationship. This involves recognizing and considering aspects such as race, gender, sexuality, socioeconomic status, and disability, among others. Intersectionality plays a vital role in shaping an individual's experiences and perspectives, and as a mentor, it is essential to acknowledge and appreciate these intersections. By deepening your understanding of your mentee's unique journey and the challenges they may face, you can provide tailored guidance and support that addresses their specific needs. This commitment to understanding and embracing intersectionality fosters a mentorship environment that values diversity, promotes equity, and facilitates the holistic development of your mentee.

Additional, tangible ways to engage in reciprocity in your liberationship is to share relevant resources, networks, and opportunities with your mentee. Introduce them to relevant workshops, conferences, or organizations that can enhance their professional development. Help them build a network of supportive individuals who can contribute to their growth and advancement. This helps to share your cultural capital with them so they can benefit from the lessons you've learned and the relationships you've cultivated throughout your career.

Resistance

Resistance of White supremacy ways of being within your mentorship relationship and beyond is a critical factor of achieving the growth, validation, and increased work productivity/contribution promised by the liberationships model. Familiarize yourself with the systemic barriers that marginalized individuals may face in higher education. Be aware of factors such as discrimination, bias, lack of representation, and unequal access to resources. Understand the intersectionality of your mentee's identities and the unique challenges they may encounter. When mentoring someone and working to resist White supremacy ways of being in your relationship and within the university or organizational institution, your mentorship relationship is being developed within, here are some strategies you can employ:

Education and awareness is a critical first step to engaging in resistance within your mentorship relationship as it can form the foundation for cultivating empathy and perspective-taking within your relationship. Help the person you're mentoring understand the historical and social context of White supremacy, its impact on marginalized communities, and the ways it perpetuates inequality. Encourage them to educate themselves through reading, documentaries, and engaging with diverse perspectives. If you yourself do not feel capable of providing this education based on your current knowledge, do not be afraid to disclose to your mentee that you are also working on expanding your understanding of these concepts. You can also engage in shared reading or training opportunities. Additionally, engaging in open and honest conversations about biases and stereotypes that they may hold can help hold space to question those assumptions and find new beliefs that are more affirmative of our multicultural world. Encourage critical thinking and questioning of assumptions. Provide counter-narratives and examples that challenge harmful stereotypes.

As you support efforts to create inclusive policies and practices in your personal and professional lives, share about this work with your mentee. If you participate in opportunities to advocate for social justice, encourage your mentee to engage alongside you, as appropriate, and speak out against injustice and discrimination. Support their engagement in social justice activities, such as attending rallies, participating in community initiatives, or joining advocacy groups that work to dismantle White supremacy. Know that acknowledging their efforts is providing validation. Seek to demonstrate inclusive behaviors and attitudes in your own interactions with others around your mentor to show them how they may engage in a multicultural space. Model empathy, respect, and fairness. Show them that resisting White supremacy is not just an abstract concept but a tangible commitment in your own life.

Another way you can practice resistance within your mentorship relationship is to share privileges and knowledge you've gained that may help your mentee engage in spaces that may expose them to new professional or personal development opportunities. Help them access networks, scholarships, internships, and other forms of support that can level the playing field and broaden their horizons. If you are able to bring them to a staff meeting, introduce them to colleagues, or nominate them for committees you serve on to further their experiences, do so. Seek to introduce them to individuals who can support their goals and aspirations. Recognize and address systemic barriers that may hinder your mentee's progress to reach their goals. Actively seek out and provide your mentee with information, resources, and opportunities that can enhance their educational and professional journey. Advocate for their access to resources, opportunities, and networks. Use your position and influence to create inclusive spaces and challenge inequitable practices. By actively working towards access and equity, you contribute to the transformative potential of the mentorship model on a systemic level.

Additionally, we recommend that you seek to acknowledge and critically reflect on your own privileges and power dynamics within the mentorship relationship. Be mindful of any unconscious biases or assumptions you may hold. Strive to create an equitable and inclusive mentorship environment that values the diverse experiences and perspectives of your mentee. If necessary, discuss these feelings and any associated questions or concerns you have with your colleagues or any mentorship program coordinators you have support from. Continuing to engage in your own awareness and understanding of ways to engage in resistance of White supremacy ways of being is an ongoing journey. Collaborate with other mentors, faculty members, administrators, and support staff to create a more inclusive and equitable academic environment. Participate in initiatives and committees that focus on diversity, equity, and inclusion. Advocate for policy changes that promote access and equity for marginalized individuals. Attend trainings and read articles that challenge your own beliefs and further your knowledge of multicultural issues.

Remember, resisting White supremacy ways of being within your mentorship relationship and any shared organizations you two are a part of is an ongoing process that requires dedication, humility, and a willingness to learn and grow. We encourage you and your mentee to be patient with this process and to continually strive for progress, not perfection. Remember to include all three key factors of reflection, reciprocity, and resistance in your interactions. As you do this work, if it feels challenging or new, be sure to share about your thoughts and feelings with your mentee to demonstrate the inner experience of engaging in such resistance.

Reflection Questions

As you prepare for your mentorship experience, consider these questions aligned with the model:

- Who
  - Who are you working with? How will you find shared identity? What identities might be shared?
  - How will you engage about desires for growth (mentees hopeful experiences through life, how mentees want to engage with the world, if through a specific program—the program outcomes)?
  - How will you acknowledge power (your positionality, systems of oppression)?
- How
  - How will you engage in reflection? What questions might you ask?
  - How will you approach reciprocity? What will you do to learn from mentees you are working with?
  - How will you cultivate resistance?
- Why
  - What growth are you hoping mentees you work with gain? What growth are you hoping you gain?
  - What validation are you hoping the mentees you are working with will feel? What validation are you hoping you feel?
  - In what ways could you and your mentees contribute to your sphere of influence and the world?

Section 2: Considerations and Recommendations for Mentees

Reflection

As a mentee, we highly recommend that you take an active role in your mentorship journey to ensure you get the most out of it. This starts by viewing yourself as worthy of having a say in how the relationship with your mentor is formed over time. During the beginning of your relationship, be sure to share about what you are interested in and what your goals are. Take ownership of your personal and professional growth by sharing openly about that which you desire to achieve. Set goals that align with your aspirations and actively work towards them by sharing about them with your mentor. Practice self-advocacy by articulating your needs and aspirations to your mentor and asking what they can do to support you or if they know others they can refer you to connect with.

Actively seek guidance and feedback from your mentor. Engage in regular discussions to reflect on your progress, address challenges, and explore strategies for improvement. Be receptive to constructive criticism and use it as an opportunity for growth. Embrace a growth mindset, viewing challenges as opportunities for learning and development. Know that you are not alone in navigating any challenges or concerns that come up for you, and reach out to your mentor proactively as you need support or have topics you'd like to learn more about with them.

Establish a collaborative and respectful relationship with your mentor. Communicate openly, express your concerns, and seek guidance when needed. Embrace feedback as a tool for growth and improvement. By actively participating in the mentorship relationship, you maximize the transformative potential of the model. To do this, try to mindfully share that which you are unsure if you can share. As needed, be sure to ask your mentor about the boundaries of communication that they feel are necessary. Clarify if you can ask about topics that feel important to you but have not been brought up yet. Know that you deserve to get what you want and need out of your mentorship relationship, and that this will only be possible if you express your needs, and a way for you to do that is by reflecting on your experiences with your mentor.

If it is not a part of the structure within your mentorship program, be sure to take time to identify your goals, both short-term and long-term, and communicate them to your mentor. Reflecting about your interests and goals will help guide your mentorship journey and provide a greater context for your mentor to better support you. Articulating your needs, expectations, and aspirations to your mentor is a skill that may take time to cultivate. Be open and honest about the support you would appreciate, whether it's academic guidance, career advice, networking opportunities, or personal development. Reflections about your goals and open communication will ensure that your mentor is aware of your specific needs and can provide tailored support so you have a more positive experience and achieve greater outcomes. Regularly evaluate your progress and adjust your approach accordingly. Consider journaling, self-assessment exercises, or seeking feedback from your mentors to aid in your self-reflection skills.

As you notice characteristics, support methods, or other things you may feel gratitude or appreciation about your mentor, acknowledge and appreciate them via reflection to you mentor. Consider the time, support, and guidance provided by your mentor, and notice if/when your relationship shifts and changes. Express awareness of, and gratitude towards for their investment in your growth and success as you feel it. This fosters a positive and mutually beneficial mentorship relationship centered on what is mutually enjoyed by both of you. As a mentee, you deserve to have a positive mentorship relationship and that is more likely to occur if you share what you do and don't appreciate. Reflecting on what you have experienced, noticed, and desire for the future will help you to actualize it in your mentorship relationship and beyond. Practicing speaking your truth and advocating for yourself with your mentor will improve your ability to do so in a variety of areas of your life.

Reciprocity

Within the liberationships model, we advise both parties to share their knowledge, power, and privileges with one another to further both of your progress towards your goals, as we believe both mentor and mentee have much to contribute to one another. This approach requires mentees to also acknowledge all that they bring to your relationship based on your past experiences. Your mentor will have much to share with you, but do not discount that which you can share with your mentor, and take initiative to vocalize your ideas and insights to them. Reciprocity in action is most possible when you maintain regular contact with your mentor, schedule meetings or check-ins, and respond promptly to their communications so that you two can engage in conversation as situations are unfolding, or quickly after.

Seek feedback from your mentor and utilize their guidance to develop new skills and expand your knowledge. Pay attention to their advice, suggestions, and feedback. Demonstrate your engagement by asking questions, seeking clarification, and reflecting on their insights. Embrace opportunities for networking, training, and community engagement to enhance your overall educational experience that they may invite you to participate in together. As you learn more about your mentor throughout your relationship, you can also take the initiative to research and explore relevant literature, workshops, conferences, or extracurricular activities that they may appreciate based on the goals they've expressed to you, which you can engage on together to enhance your learning experience.

Take advantage of networking opportunities within your field of interest that your mentor may invite you to. Attend conferences, workshops, or professional events to connect with peers and professionals who can provide valuable insights and support. Cultivating your relationship with your mentor who can offer guidance and open doors to new opportunities through reciprocity means that you will also share guidance and ideas as you are able to support your mentor, too. Collaborate with your mentor to co-create a learning plan that aligns with both of your needs and goals.

As showcased, the liberationships model emphasizes the importance of reciprocity, or mutual growth and collaboration, between mentors and mentees by each party sharing that which they can contribute to supporting each other. Recognizing that both parties have valuable knowledge, power, and privileges to contribute, this approach encourages mentees to acknowledge and appreciate their own unique experiences and insights. By actively engaging in feedback and guidance from their mentors, mentees can develop new skills, expand their knowledge, and enhance their overall educational experience. As the mentor and mentee cultivate their relationship, reciprocity plays a vital role in sharing guidance and ideas, creating a collaborative learning plan that addresses both parties' needs and goals. Embracing this symbiotic approach to mentorship leads to meaningful growth, validation, and the realization of shared professional and personal contributions.

Resistance

Engaging in resistance against White supremacy, ways of being within your mentorship relationship and beyond is crucial for achieving the growth, validation, and increased work productivity promised by the liberationships model. Reciprocity in mentorship relationships is not limited to the mentor providing guidance and support. As a mentee, you also have a valuable role to play in fostering reciprocity and contributing to the growth of the relationship. You bring a unique set of skills, insights, and ideas to the relationship based on your background and journey. Take initiative in vocalizing your ideas, sharing relevant resources or articles, and offering your perspectives on topics of mutual interest. This reciprocity allows both you and your mentor to learn from one another, fostering a reciprocal exchange of knowledge and growth.

As a mentee, it is important to familiarize yourself with the systemic barriers that marginalized individuals may face and be aware of factors such as discrimination, bias, lack of representation, and unequal access to resources. Engaging in opportunities to further explore the intersectionality of your own identities and the unique challenges you may encounter can provide valuable insights for both personal growth and the mentorship relationship as a whole. For example, let's say you identify as a woman of color pursuing a career in a male-dominated field. Through your experiences, you may have encountered various forms of bias and stereotypes, as well as limited access to resources and opportunities. By reflecting on these challenges and sharing them with your mentor, you create an opportunity to deepen your understanding of the systemic barriers at play and collectively strategize ways to navigate them through them sharing what they've learned and exhibiting reciprocity. Your mentor, equipped with their knowledge and experience, can offer guidance and support tailored to your specific circumstances. Together, you can explore approaches to address bias, advocate for inclusivity, and seek out networks and resources that can empower you to overcome the barriers that may stand in your way. This collaborative process not only strengthens your mentorship relationship but also enables you to actively contribute to dismantling systemic barriers and creating a more equitable environment for future generations of mentees.

To effectively resist White supremacy ways of being in your mentorship relationship, education and awareness serve as a critical first step. Take the initiative to understand the historical and social context of White supremacy, its impact on marginalized communities, and how it perpetuates inequality. Ask your mentor to share resources such as books, documentaries, and diverse perspectives for self-education. If your mentor feels unable to provide this education based on their current knowledge, appreciate their honesty and consider engaging in shared reading or training opportunities together. Engage in open and honest conversations about biases and stereotypes, questioning assumptions and seeking counter-narratives that challenge harmful beliefs. Share about learning opportunities or resources that you think your mentor may appreciate, and explain why or how you think it could help them to reach their goals. This demonstrates your efforts to engage in reciprocity and share of your knowledge, time, and resources with your mentor.

Support efforts to create inclusive policies or practices in your personal and professional life, and share this work with your mentor. If you are unsure of what these could be, ask your mentor for ideas of ways to navigate any situations in which you wish there were more access or less barriers. As you participate in opportunities to advocate for social justice, and encourage your mentor to join you as appropriate. Recognize and validate your own efforts and seek to demonstrate inclusive behaviors and attitudes in your interactions with others, including your mentor. Seek to improve and model empathy, respect, and fairness, showing that resistance against White supremacy is a tangible commitment in your own life. Engage in ongoing awareness and understanding of resistance against White supremacy ways of being, collaborating with others to create a more inclusive and equitable environment. Participate in initiatives, committees, and training focused on diversity, equity, and inclusion as they are presented to you and ask your mentor to participate as relevant.

Remember, engaging in resistance against White supremacy ways of being is an ongoing process that requires dedication, humility, and a willingness to learn and grow. Be patient with yourself and your mentor as you navigate this journey, striving for progress rather than perfection. Be open to receiving constructive criticism and suggestions for improvement, and try to approach your conversations with a willingness to learn and grow from your mentor's expertise and experience. Ensure that your interactions encompass reflection, reciprocity, and resistance, and share your thoughts and feelings with your mentor to demonstrate the transformative inner experience of engaging in this resistance.

In this chapter, we have presented a comprehensive guide for implementing the transformative mentorship model, focusing on considerations and recommendations for both mentors and mentees. By aligning each recommendation with the different layers of the model, we emphasize the significance of each aspect and provide practical guidance for individuals engaging in mentorship relationships. By embracing this model, mentors and mentees can foster transformative and empowering mentorship journeys, leading to personal growth, academic success, and systemic change within higher education.

Throughout this chapter, we have underscored the importance of transformative and liberatory relationships in empowering marginalized individuals and dismantling oppressive systems. We have emphasized the role of mentorship in fostering inclusive and equitable academic environments where individuals can thrive and contribute their unique perspectives and talents. By embracing cultural humility, nurturing self-reflection, and advocating for access and equity, mentors can create a safe and trusting space for their mentees to grow and excel. Similarly, mentees who actively engage in their mentorship journey, build supportive relationships, embrace personal and professional development, and cultivate resilience and self-care, can maximize the benefits of mentorship and pave the way for their own success.

In conclusion, we encourage both mentors and mentees to continue growing and expanding their knowledge of ways to engage in liberationships. We also hope that mentees will pay it forward by becoming mentors themselves one day. By sharing their experiences, insights, and knowledge, they can contribute to the transformative potential of the mentorship model and create a ripple effect of positive change within higher education. Let us celebrate the power of mentorship, recognizing its capacity to empower individuals, challenge inequities, and foster a more inclusive and equitable future. Together, we can create a supportive and nurturing academic community where every individual, regardless of their background, can thrive and contribute to a more diverse and vibrant higher education landscape.

7

Self-Reflection Activities and Worksheets

Application of the model to enhance relationships is our goal. This chapter will provide tangible resources to incorporate the liberatory mentorship for women of color model into relationship development. In this chapter you'll find worksheets, reflection activities related to one's social identities, values, personal and professional goals, relationship self-care needs, and a rubric to identify what your preferences for mentorship relationship interactions are.

Activity 1: Critical Mentorship as Women of Color in Higher Education Worksheet

(This can be done as an individual and/or in a liberationship group)

- Who
  - Reflect on your mentorship experiences.

- Where are there shared values represented in your relationship?
- What are your salient identities at work?
- How
  - What are your beliefs about the roles and expectations of a mentor and mentees?
  - How should vulnerability and reflection show up in mentor relationships?
  - How are boundaries set in mentorship relationships?
- Why
  - What personal growth are you most interested in prioritizing at this time?
  - What areas of your identity do you feel could benefit from increased validation?
  - What work/passion projects would you like to see an increased contribution in?
- Moving forward
  - Who might you want to develop a mentorship relationship with to reach your goals?
  - How would you like your mentorship relationship interactions to go?
  - What growth, validation, and increased contributions are you seeking?
  - What current projects can you apply what you learned about this model?

Activity 2: Personal Reflection Questions

- What personal growth are you most interested in prioritizing at this time?
- What are your salient identities? How are your salient identities impacted at or through work? What areas of your identity do you feel could benefit from increased validation?
- What work/passion projects would you like to see increased contributions in?
- What growth, validation, and increased contributions are you seeking?
- Who might you want to develop a mentorship relationship with to reach your goals?
- What will you need to feel supported through mentorship?
- How would you like your mentorship relationship interactions to go?

Activity 3: Journal and Reflection Prompts

These journal prompts support one's ability to reflect, which is an important aspect of liberationships. As such, here are some suggested prompts to choose to engage within your liberationship group. Choose a prompt or question for your next meeting. Reflect on it separately before your meeting. During your meeting, share what you reflected on and learned about yourself together. What did you learn from your conversation?

- Letter to your 80 year-old self
- What does your ideal work day look like?
- What does your ideal free-from-work day look like?
- If there were no rules to follow or previous commitments you had to keep, how would you spend next week? Why those things?
- If your office could not have typical office items like a desk, chair, and bookshelf in it, what would you put in it? What would it feel like?
- You're creating Starbucks' new drink, designed to make you happy. What's in it?
- You have to introduce yourself to a new group of people with a playlist. What songs are you adding and why?
- Describe a moment when you felt a strong sense of belonging. What factors contributed to that feeling?
- Reflect on a time when you overcame a significant challenge or obstacle. What strengths and resources did you draw upon to overcome it?
- Imagine you have the opportunity to have a conversation with a role model or someone you admire. What questions would you ask them and why?
- What are three core values that guide your life decisions? How do these values shape your actions and priorities?
- Write about a book, movie, or artwork that deeply resonated with you. What aspects of it touched you and why?
- Reflect on a time when you had to step outside of your comfort zone. What did you learn from that experience, and how did it contribute to your personal growth?
- Think about a place in nature that brings you a sense of peace and tranquility. Describe that place in detail and explore why it holds significance for you.
- If you had unlimited resources and time, what cause or issue would you dedicate yourself to, and how would you make a difference?

Self-Reflection Activities and Worksheets ▪ **85**

- Reflect on a skill or talent that you would like to develop or improve. Why is it important to you, and what steps can you take to work towards mastery?
- Write a letter to your future self, envisioning where you would like to be in 5 years. Describe your accomplishments, personal growth, and the impact you hope to have on others.

These journal prompts can help you explore different aspects of your life, values, aspirations, and personal experiences. They encourage self-reflection, introspection, and creative thinking. Feel free to adapt them to suit your individual preferences and interests.

Activity 4: Personal Identity Exploration

Name: _____ Date: _____

If you are engaging in a liberationship, you are continuing to grow and develop. As such, each time you engage in this Personal Identity Exploration, date it. You'll be able to come back to this and see how you've grown over the course of years which can also help you understand more about yourself, your journey, and your liberationship.

Social Identity Categories

For each of these, indicate what you identify as your social identities currently:

- Race/ethnicity:

- Gender identity:

- Sexual orientation:

- Socioeconomic status:

- Ability/disability:

- Religion/spirituality:

- Nationality/citizenship:

- Other relevant social identity categories:

Reflection Prompts

- How does your race/ethnicity influence your experiences within higher education?

- How does your gender identity impact your interactions with peers, mentors, and faculty?

- In what ways does your sexual orientation shape your sense of belonging and inclusion in educational settings?

- How does your socioeconomic status impact your access to resources and opportunities?

- How does your ability or disability influence your experiences with accessibility and accommodation?

- How does your religion or spirituality intersect with your educational journey?

- How does your nationality or citizenship status affect your experiences in higher education?

- Are there any other social identity categories that are significant to your experiences within higher education?

Intersectionality Exploration

- Reflect on how your different social identities intersect and influence each other within the context of higher education. How do these intersections shape your experiences, challenges, and perspectives?

Goal and Perspective Reflection

- How do your social identities influence your goals and aspirations within higher education?

- In what ways do your social identities provide unique perspectives and insights that contribute to your educational journey?

Additional Notes or Reflections

Use this space to jot down any additional thoughts, reflections, or insights related to your social identities and their impact on your experiences within higher education.

Reflections After Liberationship Conversation

Use this space to write down any further thoughts, reflections, or insights related to your social identities and this worksheet after engaging in conversation with those you are in a liberationship with.

Activity 5: Values Assessment

Reflect on your personal values. Consider how your values align with your educational and professional goals and how you can integrate them into your mentorship relationships. This activity is designed to help you establish a foundation for meaningful and authentic connections.

Values Identification

Look at this list of values and indicate your top 10 values. Alternatively, you can journal and articulate your top 8–10 values.

knowledge	moral fulfillment
intellectually challenging	stability
creativity	power and authority
independence	supervision
aesthetics	time freedom
intellectual status	recognition
excitement	advancement
helps others/society	money (high salary)
exercise competence	community
security	fast paced
job tranquility	deadlines/under pressure
work environment	precision work
work alone	physically challenging
public contact	fun/happiness
change and variety	location
influence others	safety
status of position	education
status of company	health/wellness
adventure	justice
competitive	relationships
friendships	travel authenticity
trust	integrity
family	compassion

Once you have identified your 8–10 top values. Rank them in order of importance. This exercise helps you identify the values they hold most close to you and may want to prioritize in their mentorship relationships.

- List your ranked top values here:

Reflection on Alignment

Once you have identified your values, reflect on how these values align with your educational and professional goals. Consider how living according to these values can contribute to your personal and academic growth.

- Why are these values important to you?

- How do these values align with your educational and professional goals?

- How can these values guide your decision-making and actions within your mentorship relationships?

- Reflect on the importance of shared values in fostering meaningful and authentic connections.

- How do your values align with the values you seek in a mentor or mentee?

- In what ways can you integrate these values into your liberationship?

Integration Into Mentorship Relationships and Goal Setting

What goals can you set for yourself based on your identified values? These goals can be related to personal growth, relationship-building, liberatory relationships themselves, or professional development. How do these goals manifest in your mentorship journey?

Reflection and Discussion

Reflect on this Value Assessment and what you've contributed throughout this activity. What insights have you gained about yourself? Engage in conversation with your liberationship partner or group about each of your values and engage in building an action plan together around your collective values.

Action Plan

Create an action plan that outlines how you will all actively incorporate your values into your mentorship relationships. This plan should include specific strategies, behaviors, and/or commitments you are willing to undertake to ensure your values guide your actions.

By engaging in the Values Assessment activity, we hope you have been able to gain a deeper understanding of your personal values and how these values can guide your actions and interactions within your mentorship relationships.

Personal and Professional Goal Setting

Complete this reflective exercise in setting specific, measurable, attainable, relevant, and time-bound (SMART) goals. Consider both short-term and long-term objectives, and how your liberationship can support achieving these goals.

Activity 6: Relationship Self-Care Inventory

This Relationship Self-Care Inventory is designed to help those engaging in mentorship relationships to reflect on their individual self-care needs within their liberationships. It prompts participants to consider various aspects of well-being and provides a framework for assessing your boundaries, emotional health, and strategies for maintaining a healthy balance between your personal and professional lives. This can serve as a tool for you to assess and communicate your self-care requirements, ensuring a balanced and supportive mentorship experience.

> Boundaries—Reflect on your boundaries within the liberationship. Consider your comfort levels in sharing personal information, setting expectations for communication frequency and modes, and defining limits on your time and energy commitments within the relationship.

> Emotional well-being—Evaluate how the liberationship affects your emotional well-being. Do you feel supported, validated, and understood by those you are in the mentorship relationship with? Does the mentorship dynamic contribute positively to your overall emotional health?

> Self-care practices—Identify and prioritize self-care practices that are essential for your well-being. This can include activities such as exercise, relaxation techniques, hobbies, socializing, and engaging in activities that bring you joy and rejuvenation.

Balance—Reflect on how you are maintaining a healthy balance between your personal and professional lives. Are you allocating enough time and energy to self-care, relationships, and other important aspects of your life outside of academics?

Communication and feedback—Evaluate the effectiveness of communication within your liberationship and the availability of a feedback mechanism both positive and negative. Are your communication needs being met? Do you feel comfortable expressing their concerns or seeking clarification?

Goal alignment—Reflect on whether your mentorship goals align with your personal aspirations and values. Is the liberationship helping you progress towards their desired outcomes and if adjustments or additional support are needed?

Activity 7: Identity-Affirming Reflection

In conversation within your liberationship, explore and celebrate aspects of your identities that bring you strength and resilience. What identities have shaped your recent decisions? How do you feel about the way your identities have influenced your lifestyle? Reflect on your cultural heritage, experiences of empowerment, and the ways in which your identities contribute to your unique perspectives and talents. If you would like more structure in this activity, consider reflecting together on each of the cultural wealths identified by Yosso (2005).

Activity 8: Liberationship Preferences

Consider including the following elements to identify your preferences for liberationship interactions and engagements:

Communication Styles

- Do you prefer direct and straightforward communication or a more indirect and diplomatic approach?
- Are you comfortable with open and candid discussions, or do you prefer a more formal and professional tone?
- How do you like to receive information: verbally, in writing, or a combination of both?

Frequency of Meetings

- How often would you like to meet with your liberationship: weekly, bi-weekly, monthly, or as needed?
- Are you open to impromptu meetings or prefer scheduled appointments?
- Would you like to have a set day/time for regular meetings or prefer flexibility?

Modes of Support

- What modes of communication do you prefer for mentorship interactions: face-to-face meetings, phone calls, video calls, emails, or instant messaging?
- Are there any specific platforms or tools you prefer for virtual communication?

Preferred Feedback Mechanisms

- How do you prefer to receive feedback: verbal discussions, written feedback, or a combination of both?
- Are you comfortable with receiving constructive criticism, and how would you like it to be delivered?
- Would you like periodic formal evaluations or ongoing feedback as situations arise?

Goal Alignment

- What are your specific goals and expectations for the liberationship?
- How do you envision your liberationship supporting you in achieving your goals?
- Are there any specific areas or skills you would like your liberationship to focus on?

Preferred Liberationship Activities

- What types of activities or experiences would you find beneficial in the liberationship? For example, attending conferences, networking events, job shadowing, or collaborative projects.
- Are there any particular resources or opportunities you would like your liberationship partner(s) to share with you?

Preferred Mentoring Style

- Do you prefer a more hands-on approach where your mentor actively guides and advises you, or a more facilitative approach where your mentor encourages liberationship style with reciprocal reflection and independent decision-making?
- Are there any specific mentoring techniques or strategies you find effective or prefer?
- When do you want to check in about these as your relationship and comfort grows?

Support for Personal and Professional Development

- Are there any specific areas or skills you would like to develop during the liberationship?
- What kind of support do you expect from your liberationship in terms of professional networking, skill-building opportunities, or personal growth?

Expectations for Confidentiality

- Are there any sensitive topics or information you would like to discuss with your liberationship partner(s) that require confidentiality?
- How important is it for you to maintain confidentiality in the liberationship?

Transformative Action Plan

Given your responses and conversation above, develop a transformative action plan. For this action plan, set intentions for actively engaging in transformative liberationships together, how you will collaboratively challenge systemic barriers, and foster the development of an inclusive and empowering relationship.

By incorporating these reflective activities into your conversations, liberationship partners will have tangible resources to enhance relationships through the liberatory mentorship for women of color model. These activities encompass self-reflection, goal setting, self-care, identity affirmation, and preferences for liberationship interactions. By engaging in these reflective practices, you can deepen your understanding of yourself, establish meaningful connections with others, and create transformative liberationship journeys that align with your personal and professional aspirations. We recommend all liberationship partners engage with these self-reflection activities and workshops regularly.

98 ▪ Liberationships

Activity 9: Liberation in the Academy: Reflection Questions for Educators

Below are questions to reflect on for the implementation of the findings from Kim McAloney's (2021) dissertation for policy and practice at the departmental or institutional level followed by the individual level. You can engage with the full text of the dissertation here (https://ir.library.oregonstate.edu/concern/graduate_thesis_or_dissertations/v979v9581). Will you join us in your own liberation and the liberation for your department and institution?

Use these questions to reflect on your campus or your department. If you do not have an answer or know how your campus or department is doing, use these questions to conduct an anonymous survey of employees. As you consider the answers for these questions, also consider any data you have from campus inclusivity surveys. Many answers may be found there or data that will highlight what employees may share in the anonymous survey.

Analyzing Your Campus/Department Readiness for Implementing Study Findings

- How do you solicit and receive feedback from those you lead to ensure you are co-creating a positive work environment?
- How do you address White supremacy culture and the current and historic role racial capitalism has on your institution, department, and employees?
  - How are you mindful of personal and professional commitments when assigning work and deadlines? Do you penalize individuals when they do not adhere to strict time structures?
  - How do you support and allow for meaningful recognition of collaboration that honors valuable collaboration rather than centering individuals?

Regularly Scheduled Meetings
- Are you actively encouraging your employees to spend the time necessary to explore potential mentorship relationship fits?
- Do you allow for part of your meeting agendas to be unstructured?
- Do you address, reflect on, and make space for processing current events and social movements during staff meetings, 1–1's?
- Do you talk about White supremacy culture and the role racial capitalism has had on your institution or department culture?
- What structures are in place to include mentorship as part of employee advancement and annual reviews?

- Do you account for time spent building mentorship relationships in one's work assignment or position description?
- How do you use data from employee inclusion surveys to shift practices that are causing harm?

Unstructured Communication Strategies
- How do you support communication amongst your employees?
- Are there social media policies in place that might restrict engagement?
- Do you support relationships among employees?
- Do you offer space and time to facilitate relationships amongst staff?
- Do you monitor employees' engagements in private communication channels where they might be able to build rapport if they had privacy?
- How do you allow and protect different types of cultural communication styles in the workplace?

Work Technology for Increased Contribution
- What tools do you provide equitable access to for employees to engage with one another?
- What proactive training and support do you offer your employees to learn new technologies that could increase communication and contributions?
- What is your campus culture around virtual engagement, relationship development, and work?
- How do you support different employee's needs to leverage technology in order to do their best work? How do you support flexibility of schedules for employees based on their personal and cultural values and needs?

Activity 10: Reflection Questions to Use as You Begin Virtual Mentor or Liberationships for Implementation of Study Findings

Use these questions as you want to begin or shift a relationship to be virtual mentorships or liberationships. The first set of questions are for each member of the relationship to engage in personal reflection. These questions will help you know where you are and what you are hoping to gain from the relationship and a few things that have led you to this point. The rest of the questions can be discussed as a mentorship or liberationship unit. Use these questions to have open, honest dialogue together as you begin or shift your relationship.

Personal Reflection Questions

- What personal growth are you most interested in prioritizing at this time?

- What are your salient identities? How are your salient identities impacted at or through work? What areas of your identity do you feel could benefit from increased validation?

- What work/passion projects would you like to see increased contributions in?

- What growth, validation, and increased contributions are you seeking?

- Who might you want to develop a mentorship relationship with to reach your goals?

- What will you need to feel supported through mentorship?

- How would you like your mentorship relationship interactions to go?

Reflection Questions With Those Engaging in the Virtual Mentorship

Regularly Scheduled Meetings

- What are your interests outside of work? What keeps you busy? Tell me about yourself (your full self, not just your work self).

- How frequently would you like to meet?

- What is the best way for us to meet (virtual, in person, flexible, etc.)

- Have you engaged in virtual mentorships? If so, what was that experience like for you?

- Were there shared values represented in this relationship?

- What are your beliefs about the roles and expectations of mentorship?

- How should vulnerability and reflection show up in mentorship relationships?

- How are boundaries set in mentorship relationships?

- How will biases be mitigated and addressed?

- What do you need in order to be able to show up as your full self in this relationship?

Unstructured Communication Strategies

- Are you aware of social media policies in place that might restrict engagement?

- Can you follow one another on social media? If so, which?

- Can you share cell numbers with one another? Are you open to texting?

- If you don't feel comfortable sharing social media or cell numbers now, when can you check in again about it again?

Work Technology for Increased Contributions

- What work/passion projects would you like to see increased contributions in?

- What growth, validation, and increased contributions are you seeking?

- What institutional (work) tools do you use regularly?

- How do you engage with each of these tools?

- What does learning a new technology mean for you? What is your process?

- Are you open to trying new technologies?

Epilogue

Gunnar Whisler
University of Chicago Law School

Rough is a bit of an understatement when I think back to the beginning of my graduate program. I was floundering to find my stride in higher education, an environment I passionately believed I belonged in and had moved across the country for. I describe(d) it as trying to love something that seemed to refuse to love me back. A lesson I had learned early on as an undergraduate student taught me I desperately needed to find something or someone that would reciprocate this desire: enter Kim, Jenesis and my experience with liberationships!

I had it all planned out, my exit from my graduate program that is, but then I read an email from Kim and Jenesis looking for graduate interns to join them on a literature review quest to analyze the impacts of mentorship on people (more specifically women identifying) of color. Admittedly, I paused before I replied and expressed my excitement and interest in this opportunity. My self-awareness kicked in and I questioned if I, a White man, had any place in joining this diverse team made up of women of color. I had existed in and benefited from White dominated places my entire life and quite frankly, I was tripping over my own Whiteness. Thankfully, I got over myself enough to reach out to Kim and Jenesis and express my curiosity about the internship and am even more so thankful they were willing to let me join their team. I desperately hoped and wondered, would this be the experience that would love me back as much as I wanted to love it? Would this be the space I would find connection with others and deeper meaning to inform my growth as a professional?

Four years later and I can still confidently say this internship was one of the most defining experiences of my life. The previous statement is a big one to make, but I mean it wholeheartedly. Throughout the internship, I engaged in several activities like those presented in Chapter 7. While I never thought of myself as someone who would benefit from journaling, this specific activity quickly became my favorite aspect of the internship. Each week, the graduate interns were asked to journal about what things came up for them during the week. That might sound vague, but it really was the point: to journal about whatever truly came up, whether it was things related to the literature review research, personal day-to-day life, work, and so on. For the first time, I felt like I had space to reflect individually and then be in community with others regarding feelings I could not place, ideas that felt stifled, and identifying obstacles I was struggling to get through. For example, I journaled fairly extensively about how my various identities (some privileged and some not) as a White, cisgender, gay man from a rural and working class background played a role in my thought processes and biases as I interacted with the literature and my fellow group members (for better or for worse).

Kim and Jenesis were diligent in creating a foundation based in organic trust, genuine compassion, and mutual understanding that each person brought their own invaluable worth to the collective group and project. Being educated in the American education system, the power dynamic between mentor and mentee was always something I reckoned with. Realizing Kim and Jenesis saw me as someone who was not inferior, but someone who had their own intrinsic worth beyond what work I was capable of producing for the literature review, is a part of what healed and restored the way I viewed my own self and my work.

True to the liberationships model, the mentoring relationships I still have with both Kim and Jenesis operate through the different layers of the model as described throughout this book. Fairly quickly, we found despite the fact that on the surface people might not suspect many shared identities, we did have much in common. I, too, came from a rural, working or lower class background. I also encountered many difficulties as a first generation student, and while I cannot claim my experiences as a gay man qualify me to understand how Kim and Jenesis are perceived and perceive the world as women of color, I had my own, different learned understanding of what it was like to be otherized. It was through this internship that we collectively realized we were organically engaging in the liberationships model of mentoring!

As I have informally walked through the "who" and the "how" of the liberationships model in terms of the liberationships I have with both Kim and Jenesis, it leads me to the "why." At the time I am writing this epilogue, it has been over four years since I participated in this graduate internship. I took on the internship opportunity to participate in a literature review, never anticipating the seemingly endless benefits that are a direct result from my time and liberationships with Kim and Jenesis. As I reflect on my time post-internship, I am filled with such a sense of joy and fondness to see how connected my continued growth as a young professional has been to this experience.

When I thought about what I wanted out of my time in my graduate program, I knew it was a goal of mine to present at a conference and to be published. My experiences with research in my undergraduate career were very similar to Jenesis's in that I was also a Psychology major (though not honors!) and was pushed to work with faculty doing quantitative research. Truthfully, I was originally taught that qualitative research was baseless and essentially useless. One of my first courses in my graduate program refuted these claims and I was only more determined to have a chance to participate in qualitative research. I could not have been more thrilled than when Kim and Jenesis presented the idea that we could "work smarter, not harder" (thank you Dr. Larry Roper for this forever quote) and use this internship as a way to accomplish those very goals of mine. We were successful in getting accepted to present at the 12th Annual Mentoring Institute at the University of New Mexico and our work was published in The Chronicle of Mentoring and Coaching. It was because we had engaged in liberationships that we also were able to succeed in a more traditional sense of mentorship in addition to the depth and holistic nature of our shared bonds.

One of the most important aspects of growth that occurred through my liberationships was my own furthered (and still continuing) development and enhancement of cultural humility, as well as how I am able to authentically champion diversity. Being able to leverage the privilege I have, speaking from the lens of my marginalized identities, and having the humility to be truly in community with others has been a powerful way to create progressive and positive changes in whatever environment I am in. This was recognized by colleagues in my first post-graduate role where I was asked to help form the beginnings of the Representative, Inclusion, and Equity Alliance, a group of staff who sought to address issues related to social justice that impacted our campus. This institution is situated in a state that is notorious for its attacks on diversity, equity and inclusion initiatives. While that institution in particular was not beholden to the state legislature, it was still a toxic environment to even just exist in, let alone try to move the proverbial ball of progress for students and the campus community as a whole. Though I have since moved on from this institution and that state, I credit the growth gained from my liberationships with Kim and Jenesis in my ability to persist and resist.

Presently, my current role as a technical staff member at a higher education institution is one that I would have never dreamed I would hold. While my liberationships with Kim and Jenesis has not taught me how to interpret SQL code for queries, it has positioned me to successfully navigate the complexities of higher education, see value in myself (first) and my work (second), and provide me with a lifelong, mutually supportive community among many other cherished insights and lessons. My continued friendship and relationship with Kim and Jenesis has led to a variety of experiences, from being in continuing conversations regarding the development of a mentoring program (for the same graduate program the three of us graduated from) to being asked to write this epilogue. I have yet to experience liberationships as not only a mentee, but as a mentor, though I fully intend to return to this book and my mentors when the time comes. Despite this, I have found that the elements of liberationship have a place in my everyday life still to this day. When I am encountering rough times, I have my liberationships and liberating experiences to guide me through. To answer my earlier question; I finally found the "something" and the "someone(s)" that love me back.

References

Agosto, V., Karanxha, Z., Unterreiner, A., Cobb-Roberts, D., Esnard, T., Wu, K., & Beck, M. (2016). Running bamboo: A mentoring network of women intending to thrive in academia. *NASPA Journal about Women in Higher Education, 9*(1), 74–89.

Aguilera, C. (2002). Fighter [Song]. On *Stripped* [Album]. Sony Music Entertainment.

Alarcón, J. D., & Bettez, S. (2017). Feeling Brown in the academy: Decolonizing mentoring through a disidentification muxerista approach. *Equity & Excellence in Education, 50*(1), 25–40. https://doi.org/10.1080/10665684.2016.1250234

Ards, A. A. (2015). *Words of witness: Black women's autobiography in the post-Brown era.* The University of Wisconsin Press.

Baszile, D. T. (2008). Beyond all reason indeed: The pedagogical promise of critical race testimony. *Race Ethnicity and Education, 11*(3), 251–265.

Baxter Magolda, M. B., & King, P. M. (2004). *Learning partnerships theory and models of practice to education for self-authorship.* Stylus.

Brooks, M. P., & Houck, D. W. (Eds.). (2011). *The speeches of Fannie Lou Hamer: To tell it like it is.* University Press of Mississippi.

Cantu, N. (2012). Getting there *cuano no hay camino* (when there is no path): Paths to discovery *testimonios* by Chicanas in STEM. *Equity & Excellence in Education. 45*(3), 72–87. http://doi.org/10.1080/10665684.2012.698936

Chaney, C., Edwards, L., Thompson-Rogers, G. K., Davis, D. J., & Gines, K. T. (2011). Academe as extreme sport: Black women, faculty development and networking. *The Negro Educational Review, 62–63*(1–4), 167–185.

Chavez, M. S. (2012). Authoethnography, a Chicana's methodological research tool: The role of storytelling for those who have no choice but to

do critical race theory. *Equity & Excellence in Education, 45*(2), 334–348. https://doi.org/10.1080/10665684.2012.669196
Chika. (2019). High rises [Song]. Warner Records.
Childers, S. M. (2014). Promiscuous analysis in qualitative research. *Qualitative Inquiry, 20*(6), 819–826.
Ciara. (2019). Melanin (feat. Lupita Nyong'o, Ester Dean, City Girls, & LALA) [Song]. Beauty Marks Entertainment.
Clayborne, H. L., & Hamrick, F. (2007). Rearticulating the leadership experiences of African American women in midlevel student affairs administration. *NASPA Journal, 44*(1), 123–146.
Collins, P. H. (1990). *Black feminist thought: Knowledge, consciousness, and the politics of empowerment.* Unwin Hyman.
Davis, A. T. (2009). Empowering African American women in higher education through mentoring. *Journal of the National Society of Allied Health, 6*(7), 53–58.
Davis, D. J., Coffee, T., Murphy, J., & Woods, J. (2014). Reflecting upon our experiences: An auto-ethnographic approach to understanding graduate learning. *Reflective Practice, 15*(5), 666–671. https//doi.org/10.1080/14623943.2014.944124
Delgado Bernal, D., Burciaga, R., & Flores Carmona, J. (2012). Chicana/Latina *testimonios*: Mapping the methodological, pedagogical, and political. *Equity & Excellence in Education, 45*(3), 363–372. https://doi.org/10.1080/10665684.2012.698149
Dillard, C. (2012). *Learning to (re)member the things we've learned to forget.* Peter Lang.
Dobson, M. (2012). Poetic inquiry. *The International Journal of the Arts in Society: Annual Review, 6*(5), 129–138.
Educational Opportunities Program. (2021). *About EOP.* Retrieved on January 6, 2022, from https://eop.oregonstate.edu/griggs/eop#about
Edwards, K. T. (2013). Fluidity and possibility: Imagining women of colour pedagogies. In N. Wane, J. Jagire, & Z. Murad (Eds.), *Ruptures: Anti-colonial & anti-racist feminist theorizing* (pp. 139–156). Sense Publishers.
Ek, L. D., Quijada Cerecer, P., Alanís, I., & Rodríguez, M. A. (2010). "I don't belong here": Chicanas/Latinas at a Hispanic serving institution creating community through muxerista mentoring. *Equity & Excellence in Education, 43*(4), 539–553.
Erikson, E. H. (1968). *Identity: Youth and crisis.* Norton.
Evans, S. Y. (2007). *Black women in the ivory tower, 1850–1954: An intellectual history* (1st ed.). University Press of Florida.
Fanon, F. F. (1963). *The wretched of the earth.* Kwela Books.
Flores Carmona, J. (2018). Pedagogical border crossings: Testimonio y reflexiones de una Mexicana académica. *Journal of Latinos and education. 17*(1), 92–97.
Friere, P. (1970). *Pedagogy of the oppressed.* Herder and Herder.

Gall, M. D., Gall, Joyce P., & Borg, W. R. (2007). *Educational research: An introduction* (8th ed.). Pearson/Allyn & Bacon.

Galvin, K., & Prendergast, M. (2016). *Poetic inquiry II: Seeing, caring, understanding: Using poetry as and for inquiry.* Sense Publishing.

Graham, P. A. (1978). Expansion and exclusion: A history of women in American higher education. *Signs: Journal of Women in Culture and Society, 3*(4), 759–773.

Gregory, S. T. (2001). Black faculty women in the academy: History, status, and future. *The Journal of Negro Education, 70*(3), 124–138. https://doi.org/10.2307/3211205

Griffin, K. (2013). Voices of the othermothers: Reconsidering Black professors' relationships with Black students as a form of social exchange. *The Journal of Negro Education, 82*(2), 169–183. https://doi.org/10.7709/jnegroeducation.82.2.0169

hooks, b. (1998). *Teaching to transgress: Education as the practice of freedom.* Routledge.

Jehangir, R. (2010). Stories as knowledge: Bringing the lived experience of first-generation college students into the academy. *Urban Education, 45*(4), 533–553.

Jolivette, A. (2020). *Indigenous peoples' day: Honoring Black and Indigenous solidarities* [Workshop for OSU]. Retrieved from https://doi.org/10.1177/0042085910372352

Kram, K. E. (1985). *Mentoring at work: Developmental relationships in organizational life.* University Press of America.

Lent, R. W., Brown, S. D., & Hackett, G. (1994). Toward a unifying social cognitive theory of career and academic interest, choice, and performance. *Journal of Vocational Behavior, 45*(1), 79–122.

Lincoln, C. E., & Mamiya, L. H. (1990). *The Black church in the African American experience.* Duke University Press.

Lizzo. (2019a). Exactly How I Feel [Song]. On *Cuz I Love You (Super Deluxe)* [Album]. Nice Life Recording Company and Atlantic Recording Corporation for the United States and WEA International Ince. For the world outside of the United States.

Lizzo. (2019b). Good as Hell [Song]. On *Cuz I Love You (Super Deluxe)* [Album]. Nice Life Recording Company and Atlantic Recording Corporation for the United States and WEA International Ince. For the world outside of the United States.

McAloney, K. (2021). *Virtual mentorship for women of color* [Doctoral dissertation, Oregon State University]. Oregon State University. https://ir.library.oregonstate.edu/concern/graduate_thesis_or_dissertations/v979v9581

McAloney, K., & Long, J. (2018, December 20). Transformational women of color mentorship [blog post]. Retrieved from https://owhe.org/owhe-blog/2018/12/transformative-mentorship-women-color

McAloney, K., & Long, J. (2019). Critical mentorship for women of color in higher education. *The Chronicle of Mentoring and Coaching, 3*, 77–80.

McLane-Davison, D. R., Quinn, C. R., Hardy, K., & Smith, R. L. (2017). The power of sum: An accountability sistah circle. *Journal of Social Work Education, 54*(1), 18–32.

Miller-Bernal, L., & Poulson, S. L. (2007). *Challenged by coeducation.* Vanderbilt University Press.

Nash, R. J., & Viray, S. (2013). *Our stories matter: Liberating the voices of marginalized students through scholarly personal narrative writing.* Peter Lang.

NASPA Undergraduate Fellows Program. (2021). *NASPA.* Retrieved on January 13, 2022 from https://www.naspa.org/division/naspa-undergraduate-fellows-program-nufp

Nganga, C. W., & Beck, M. (2017). The power of dialogue and meaningful connectedness: Conversations between two female scholars. *Urban Review: Issues and Ideas in Public Education, 49*(4), 551–567.

Nunez, G. G. (2014). Engaged scholarship with communities. *Journal of Hispanic Higher Education, 13*(2), 92–115. https://doi.org/10.1177/1538192713515911

Paterson, B., & Hart-Wasekeesikaw, F. (1994). Mentoring women in higher education: Lessons from the elders. *College Teaching, 42*(2), 72–77.

Peril, L. (2006). *College girls: Bluestockings, sex kittens, and coeds, then and now* (1st ed.). W. W. Norton & Co.

Pratt-Clark, M. A. E. (2014). Building a foundation for Africana sociology: Black sociology, Afrocentricity, and transdisciplinary applied social justice. *Critical Sociology, 40*(2), 217–227. https:doi.org/10.1177/0896920512443140

Prieto, L., & Villenas, S. A. (2012). Pedagogies from nepantla: Testimonio, Chicana/Latina feminisms and teacher education classrooms. *Equity & Excellence in Education, 45*(3), 411–429. https://doi.org/10.1080/10665684.2012.698197

Ragins, B. R., & Kram, K. E. (2007). *The handbook of mentoring at work: Theory, research, and practice.* SAGE.

Rapsody & Queen Latifah. (2019). Hatshepsut [Song]. On *Eve* [Album]. Jamla Records, LLC.

Rendón, L. (2008). *Sentipensante pedagogy: Sensing and thinking pedagogy.* Stylus Publishing.

Rhodes, J. E. (2002). *Stand by me: The risks and rewards of mentoring today's youth.* Harvard University Press.

Rhodes, J. E. (2005). A model of youth mentoring. In D. L. Du Bois & M. J. Karcher (Eds.), *Handbook of youth mentoring* (pp. 30–43). SAGE.

Sarasvathy, S. D. (2008). *Effectuation: Elements of entrepreneurial expertise.* Edward Elgar Publishing.

Sawyer, R. D., Norris, J. (2013). *Duoethnography.* Oxford University Press.

Schensul, J. J., & LeCompte, M. D. (2012). *Essential ethnographic methods.* RLA.

Sipe, C. L., & Roder, A. E. (2015). The effects of youth mentoring programs: A meta-analysis of outcome studies. *Journal of Community Psychology, 43*(3), 253–270.

Smitherman, G. (1977). *Talkin and testifyin: The language of Black America*. Wayne State University Press.

Snipes, J. T., & LePeau, L. A. (2017). Becoming a scholar: A duoethnography of transformative learning spaces. *International Journal of Qualitative Studies in Education, 30*(6), 575–595. https://doi.org/10.1080/09518398.2016.126972

Speedy, J. (2016). *Staring at the park: A poetic autoethnographic inquiry* (Writing lives: Ethnographic narratives). Routledge.

Squire, D. D., Kelly, B. T., Jourian, T. J., Byrd, A. M., Manzano, L. J., & Bumbry, M. (2016). A critical race feminist analysis of men of color matriculating into a higher education doctoral program. *Journal of Diversity in Higher Education, 11*(1), 16–33. https://doi.org/10.1037/dhe0000025

Thomas, G. D., & Hollenshead, C. (2001). Resisting from the margins: The coping strategies of Black women and other women of color faculty members at a research university. *The Journal of Negro Education, 70*(3), 166–175.

Wilder, C. S. (2013). *Ebony and Ivy: Race, slavery, and the troubled history of America's universities*. Bloomsberry Press.

Wilmore, G. S. (2004). *Pragmatic spirituality: The Christian faith through an Afrocentric lens*. New York University Press.

Vygotsky, L. S. (1978). *Mind in society: The development of higher psychological processes*. Harvard University Press.

Yosso, T. (2005). Whose culture has capital? A critical race theory discussion of community cultural wealth. *Race and Ethnicity in Education, 8*(1), 69–91.

Zachary, L. J. (2000). *The mentor's guide: Facilitating effective learning relationships*. Jossey-Bass.

About the Authors

Kim McAloney (she/hers) serves as the assistant professor of teaching in the CSSA program at Oregon State University. She is a scholar-practitioner change agent valuing innovation, creativity, and collaborative public pedagogy. After serving over a decade in student and academic affairs programs, Dr. Kim focus on cultivating opportunities for others through teaching, scholarship, liberationships, and coaching within and outside the academe.

Her work aims to move forward concepts of liberation, access, and equity in higher education through: educator praxis, virtual liberatory practices, liberationships/critical mentorship, first generation college students & those of us who become educators, and actualizing liberatory approaches to social change. She defines liberationships as mutually beneficial relationships that empower all parties to reach their personally-defined goals while addressing systemic barriers.

Jenesis Rose Long (she/hers) is a relationship researcher, author, coach, and podcast host. For over 6 years, Jenesis' academic and professional work has focused on the intersection of values-based decision making in career and academic pursuits and the impact of mentorship relationships for underserved populations. Alongside this work, Jenesis has taught university courses such as Career Decision Making and Business Career Management and Planning for undergraduate students, as well as Fundamentals of Counseling for graduate students pursuing work in higher education. Jenesis holds a Masters of Education in College Student Service Administration with a specialization in Program Development, as well as an honors Bachelor's of Science in Psychology, both from Oregon State University. She currently lives in South Dakota where she enjoys spending time with her family and friends, reading, painting, and walking her two dogs Molly and Dunkin'.